Maria Woods

THE GREEK PHILOSOPHERS

from Thales to Aristotle

The Greek Philosophers

from Thales to Aristotle

W. K. C. GUTHRIE

METHUEN & CO LTD
11 NEW FETTER LANE · LONDON EC4

First published 16 March 1950
Reprinted 1956 and 1962
First published in this style 1967

First published as
a University Paperback 1967
Reprinted three times
Reprinted 1978

ISBN 0 416 69700 3

Printed in Great Britain by
Fletcher & Son Ltd · Norwich

Distributed in the USA by
HARPER & ROW PUBLISHERS, INC.
BARNES & NOBLE IMPORT DIVISION

CONTENTS

CHAPTER I

GREEK WAYS OF THINKING

TO indicate the scope and aim of the following pages it will be best to say at once that they are based on a short course of lectures designed for an audience of undergraduates who were reading any subject other than Classics. It was assumed that those who were listening knew no Greek, but that an interest in some other subject, such as English, History or Mathematics (for there was at least one mathematician among them), or perhaps nothing more than general reading, had given them the impression that Greek ideas were at the bottom of much in later European thought and consequently a desire to know more exactly what these Greek ideas had been in the first place. They had, one might suppose, encountered them already, but in a series of distorting mirrors, according as this or that writer in England, Germany or elsewhere had used them for his own purposes and tinged them with the quality of his own mind and age, or, it may be, was unconsciously influenced by them in the formulation of his views. Some had read works of Plato and Aristotle in translation, and must have found parts of them puzzling because they arose out of the intellectual climate of the fourth century B.C. in Greece, whereas their readers had been led back to them from the climate of a later age and a different country.

Acting on these assumptions I tried, and shall now try for any readers who may be in a similar position, to give some account of Greek philosophy from its beginnings, to explain Plato and Aristotle in the light of their predecessors rather than their successors, and to convey some idea of the characteristic features of the Greek way of thinking and outlook on the world.[1] I shall make little or no reference to their influence on thinkers of later Europe or of our own country. This is not due only to the limitations imposed by my own ignorance, but also to a belief that it will be more enjoyable and profitable for a reader to detect such influence and draw comparisons for himself, out of his own reading and sphere of interests. My object will be, by talking about the Greeks for themselves and for their own sake, to give the material for such comparison and a solid basis on which it may rest. A certain work on Existentialism shows, so I have read, a 'genealogical tree' of the existentialist philosophy. At its root is placed Socrates, apparently on the ground that he was the author of the saying 'Know thyself'. Apart from the question whether Socrates meant by these words anything like what the twentieth-century Existentialist means, this ignores the fact that the saying was not the invention of Socrates but a proverbial piece of Greek wisdom whose author, if one must attribute it to someone, can only be said to have been the god Apollo. At any rate it was known

[1] It should be said at once that this has been done, as well as it is ever likely to be, by F. M. Cornford in *Before and After Socrates* (Cambridge University Press, 1932). The fact that this book is out of print, and under present conditions likely to remain so for some time, is the best justification for the present work. Readers who are lucky enough to obtain it, however, will find that Cornford's approach is different, and also that this book, being slightly longer, contains rather more in actual material.

to Socrates, and every other Greek, as one of the age-old precepts which were inscribed on the walls of Apollo's temple at Delphi. That it belonged to the teaching of Apolline religion is not unimportant, and the example, though small, will serve to illustrate the sort of distortion which even a brief outline of ancient thought may help to prevent.

The approach which I have suggested should have the advantage of showing up certain important differences between the Greek ways of thought and our own, which tend to be obscured when (for example) Greek atomic science or Plato's theory of the State are uprooted from their natural soil in the earlier and contemporary Greek world and regarded in isolation as the forerunners of modern atomic physics or political theory. For all the immense debt which Europe, and with Europe England, owe to Greek culture, the Greeks remain in many respects a remarkably *foreign* people, and to get inside their minds requires a real effort, for it means unthinking much that has become part and parcel of our mental equipment so that we carry it about with us unquestioningly and for the most part unconsciously. In the great days of Victorian scholarship, when the Classics were regarded as furnishing models, not only intellectual but moral, for the English gentleman to follow, there was perhaps a tendency to overemphasize similarities and lose sight of differences. The scholarship of our own day, in many respects inferior, has this advantage, that it is based both on a more intensive study of Greek habits of thought and linguistic usage and on a more extensive acquaintance with the mental equipment of earlier peoples both in Greece and elsewhere. Thanks in part to the progress of anthropology, and to the work of classical scholars acute enough to see the relevance to their studies of some of the anthropologists' results, we can claim without arrogance to be in a better position to appreciate the hidden foundations of Greek thought, the presuppositions which they accepted tacitly as we to-day accept the established rules of logic or the fact of the earth's rotation.

And here it must be said frankly, though with no wish to dwell on a difficulty at the outset, that to understand Greek ways of thinking without some knowledge of the Greek language is not easy. Language and thought are inextricably interwoven, and interact on one another. Words have a history and associations, which for those who use them contribute an important part of the meaning, not least because their effect is unconsciously felt rather than intellectually apprehended. Even in contemporary languages, beyond a few words for material objects, it is practically impossible to translate a word so as to give exactly the same impression to a foreigner as is given by the original to those who hear it in their own country. With the Greeks, these difficulties are greatly increased by the lapse of time and difference of cultural environment, which when two modern European nations are in question is so largely shared between them. When we have to rely on single-word English equivalents like 'justice' or 'virtue' without an acquaintance with the various usages of their Greek counterparts in different contexts, we not only lose a great deal of the content of the *Greek* words but import our own English associations which are often quite foreign to the intention of the Greek. It will therefore be necessary sometimes to introduce Greek terms, and explain as clearly as possible how they were used. If this should have the effect of enticing some to learn Greek, or refurbish any Greek which may have been learned at school and dropped in favour of other things, that will be all to the good. But the present account will continue on the assumption that any Greek word used needs to be explained.

Before going further, a few examples would perhaps be helpful to bring out my meaning when I say that if we want to understand an ancient Greek thinker like Plato it is important to know something of the history, affinities and usage of at any rate the most important of the terms which he employs, rather than resting content with loose English equivalents like 'justice', 'virtue', and 'god', which are all that we find in most translations. I cannot begin better than by a quotation from Cornford's preface to his own translation of the *Republic*:

> Many key-words, such as 'music', 'gymnastic', 'virtue', 'philosophy', have shifted their meaning or acquired false associations for English ears. One who opened Jowett's version at random and lighted on the statement (at 549 b) that the best guardian for a man's 'virtue' is 'philosophy tempered with music', might run away with the idea that, in order to avoid irregular relations with women, he had better play the violin in the intervals of studying metaphysics. There may be some truth in this; but only after reading widely in other parts of the book would he discover that it was not quite what Plato meant by describing *logos*, combined with *musike*, as the only sure safeguard of *arete*.

Let us take three terms which will be generally agreed to stand for concepts fundamental in the writings of any moral or metaphysical philosopher in which they occur—the words which we translate respectively as 'justice', 'virtue', and 'god'.

The word translated 'justice' is *dike*, from which comes an adjective *dikaios*, 'just', and from that again a longer form of the noun, *dikaiosyne*, 'the state of being *dikaios*'. The last word is the one generally used by Plato in the famous discussion of the nature of 'justice' in the *Republic*.

Now the original meaning of *dike* may have been literally a way or path. Whether or not that is its etymological origin, its earliest significance in Greek literature is certainly no more than the way in which a certain class of people usually behaves, or the normal course of nature. There is no implication that it is the right way, nor does the word contain any suggestion of obligation. In the *Odyssey*, when Penelope is reminding the servants what a good master Odysseus was, she says that he never did or said anything that was cruel or overweening, nor did he have favourites, 'as is the *dike* of lords'—i.e. it is the way they are wont to behave. When Eumaeus the swineherd entertains his master unawares, he apologizes for the simplicity of his fare by saying: 'What I offer is little, though willingly given, for that is the *dike* of serfs like myself, who go ever in fear.' It is, he means, the normal thing, what is to be expected. Describing a disease, the medical writer Hippocrates says, 'Death does not follow these symptoms in the course of *dike*', meaning simply, 'does not normally follow'.[1]

It was easy for such a word to slip from this purely

[1] *Odyssey*, iv, 689 ff., xiv, 58 ff.; Hippocrates, *de volneribus capitis* 3.

non-moral sense of what was to be expected in the normal course of events, and to take on something of the flavour which we imply when we speak of 'what is expected of a man', i.e. that he will act decently, pay his debts and so forth. This transition came about early, and in the poetry of Aeschylus, a century before Plato, Dike is already personified as the majestic spirit of righteousness seated on a throne by the side of Zeus. Yet it is impossible that the earlier meaning of the word should have ceased to colour the minds of the men who used it, and who as children had learned to read from the pages of Homer. Indeed a kind of petrified relic remained throughout in the use of the accusative, *diken*, as a preposition to mean 'like' or 'after the manner of'.

At the conclusion of the attempts to define 'justice' in the *Republic*, after several definitions have been rejected which more or less correspond to our notions of what we mean by the word, the one which is finally accepted is this: justice, *dikaiosyne*, the state of the man who follows *dike*, is no more than 'minding your own business', doing the thing, or following the way, which is properly your own, and not mixing yourself up in the ways of other people and trying to do their jobs for them. Does it sometimes seem to us rather a mouselike result to be born of such mountains of discussion? If so, it may make it a little more interesting to reflect that what Plato has done is to reject the meanings of the word which were current in his own day, and with a possibly unconscious historical sense to go back to the original meaning of the word. It was rooted in the class-distinctions of the old Homeric aristocracy, where right action was summed up in a man's knowing his proper place and sticking to it, and to Plato, who was founding a new aristocracy, class-distinctions—based this time on a clearly thought-out division of functions determined by psychological considerations, but class-distinctions nevertheless—were the mainstay of the state.

Our second example is the word generally rendered 'virtue'. This is *arete.* It is used in the plural as well as the singular, and the first thing to grasp about it is that, as Aristotle said, it is a relative term, not one used absolutely as the English 'virtue' is. *Arete* meant being good *at* something, and it was natural for a Greek on hearing the word to ask: 'The *arete* of what or whom?' It is commonly followed by a dependent genitive or a limiting adjective. (I make no apology for introducing these grammatical terms, for the point I want to bring home is that grammar and thought, language and philosophy, are inextricably intertwined, and that, while it is only too easy to dismiss something as 'a purely linguistic matter', there can in fact be no such thing as a divorce between the expression of a thought and its content.) *Arete* then is a word which by itself is incomplete. There is the *arete* of wrestlers, riders, generals, shoemakers, slaves. There is political *arete*, domestic *arete*, military *arete.* It meant in fact 'efficiency'. In the fifth century B.C. a class of itinerant teachers arose, the Sophists, who claimed to impart *arete*, especially that of the politician and the public speaker. This did not mean that their teaching was primarily ethical, though the more conservative of them certainly included morality in their conception of political virtue. What they wished to emphasize was its practical and immediately useful nature.

Arete was vocational, and the correspondence course in business efficiency, had it existed in ancient Greece, would undoubtedly have had the word *arete* prominently displayed in its advertisements.

It could of course be used by itself when there was no doubt of the meaning. So used it would be understood to stand for the kind of excellence most prized by a particular community. Thus among Homer's warrior-chiefs it stood for valour. Its use by Socrates, Plato, and Aristotle had an element of novelty. They qualified it by the adjective *anthropine*, 'human', thus giving it a general sense—the excellence of a man as such, efficiency in living—and surprised people by suggesting that they did not know what this was, but that it was something which must be searched for. The search meant—note the legacy of *arete* as a word of *practical* import—the discovery of the function—*ergon*, the work or job—of man. Just as a soldier, a politician and a shoemaker have a certain function, so, they argued, there must be a general function which we all have to perform in virtue of our common humanity. Find that out, and you will know in what human excellence or *arete* consists. This generalization, which alone brings the meaning of the word anywhere near to that of 'virtue', was to some extent an innovation of the philosophers, and even with them the influence of its essentially practical import never disappeared.

Arete then meant first of all skill or efficiency at a particular job, and it will be agreed that such efficiency depends on a proper understanding or knowledge of the job in hand. It is not therefore surprising that when the philosophers generalized the notion to include the proper performance of his function by any human being as such, its connexion with knowledge should have persisted. Everyone has heard of the 'Socratic paradox', his statement that 'virtue is knowledge'. Perhaps it begins to look a little less paradoxical when we see that what it would naturally mean to a contemporary was more like: 'You can't be efficient unless you take the trouble to learn the job.'

The third example is the Greek word for god—*theos*. When we are trying to understand Plato's religious views, we as students of religion or philosophy attach importance to the question of whether he was a polytheist or a monotheist—two words invented, from Greek roots indeed, but in modern times, to cover a modern, non-Greek classification. We compare the words of Plato (often in translation) with those of Christian, Indian or other theologians. But perhaps it is even more important to take account of his native language, bearing in mind a good point made by the German scholar Wilamowitz that *theos*, the Greek word which we have in mind when we speak of Plato's god, has primarily a predicative force. That is to say, the Greeks did not, as Christians or Jews do, first assert the existence of God and then proceed to enumerate his attributes, saying 'God is good', 'God is love' and so forth. Rather they were so impressed or awed by the things in life or nature remarkable either for joy or fear that they said 'this is a god' or 'that is a god'. The Christian says 'God is love', the Greek 'Love is *theos*', or 'a god'. As another writer has explained it: 'By saying that love, or victory, is god, or, to be more accurate, a god, was meant first and foremost that it is more than human, not subject to death, everlasting . . . Any power, any force we see at work in the world, which is not born with us and will continue after we are gone could thus be called a god, and most of them were.'[1]

In this state of mind, and with this sensitiveness to the superhuman character of many things which happen to us, and which give us, it may be, sudden stabs of joy or pain which we do not understand, a Greek poet could write lines like: 'Recognition between friends is *theos*'. It is a state of mind which obviously has no small bearing on the much-discussed question of monotheism or polytheism in Plato, if indeed it does not rob the question of meaning altogether. Cornford in his inaugural lecture at Cambridge remarked that philosophical discussion in any given epoch is governed to a surprising extent by a set of assumptions which are seldom or never mentioned. These assumptions are 'that groundwork of current conceptions shared by all men of any given culture and never mentioned because it is taken for granted as obvious'. He quotes Whitehead as writing: 'When you are criticizing the philosophy of an epoch, do not chiefly direct your attention to those intellectual positions which its exponents feel it necessary explicitly to defend. There will be some fundamental assumptions which adherents of all the variant systems within the epoch unconsciously presuppose.'

That is where a knowledge of the language comes in. By studying the ways in which the Greeks used their words—not only the philosophers, but poets and orators and historians in a variety of contexts and situations—we are able to get a certain insight

[1] G. M. A. Grube, *Plato's Thought* (Methuen, 1935), p. 150.

into the unconscious presuppositions of the epoch in which they lived.

As another example of the unconscious presuppositions of the epoch, we may remind ourselves how close were the Greeks in early times, and many of the common people throughout the classical period, to the magical stage of thought. Magic is a primitive form of applied science. Whether or not spirits or gods are thought to enter at some stage into the process, their actions are compelled by the man in possession of the proper magical technique no less than if they were inanimate objects. The sorcerer sets in train a certain sequence of events, and cause and effect then follow with the same certainty as if one took good aim with a rifle and pulled the trigger. Applied science is based on laws of nature. So was magic, though its laws were such as we have ceased to believe in. Fundamental was the law of sympathy, which posited a natural connexion between certain things which to us seem to have no such connexion at all. Its effect was that where two things are thus connected, then whatever one of them does or suffers the other will inevitably do or suffer too. This sort of connexion exists between a man and his image or portrait. It exists also between the man and anything which once was part of him like hair-trimmings or nail-parings, or even clothes which through close contact have become charged with his personality. Hence the well-known practices of ill-treating a doll which has been given the name of an enemy, or burning (with the proper incantations) his hair or a thread of his coat. Sympathy exists moreover between things or people and their names. Even to write the name of an enemy on a lead plate, transfix it and bury it (thus consigning it to the powers of the underworld), could injure or kill him. This is a practice which, though primitive in the extreme, was rife in the neighbourhood of Athens itself in the fourth century B.C., that is, in the lifetimes of Plato and Aristotle.

To people who think like this, the name is clearly as real as the thing, and belongs very closely to it. 'A name', as somebody has said, 'is as much a part of a person as a limb.' Now Plato's dialogue *Cratylus* deals with the origin of language, and is largely concerned with the question whether the names of things belong to them 'by nature' or 'by convention', whether they are attached as a natural part of the thing or only arbitrarily imposed by man. The question sounds nonsensical, and there seems to be a thick screen between us and people who could spend hours discussing it. But it becomes more interesting in the light of what I have been saying, and of the works of anthropologists like those of the French school represented by Lévy-Bruhl, who argues for what he calls the pre-logical mentality of primitive man, a stage of human development when the actual processes of thought are different from ours and what we call logic has no place. He has been criticized for this, and I think rightly. It is not that the human mind ever worked on entirely different lines, but simply that in the then state of knowledge the premises from which men reasoned were so different that they inevitably came to what are in our eyes very odd conclusions. The results are the same in either case. Certain things are connected or even identified in their minds in what we regard as an unreasonable way. The point of view of

Cratylus in Plato's dialogue betrays just the state of mind in which magical association is possible when he says: 'It seems to me quite simple. The man who knows the names knows the things.' Socrates asks him if he is to understand him as meaning that the man who has discovered a name has discovered the thing of which it is the name, and he agrees that that is exactly what he wants to convey. It is interesting how, when he is driven back by the argument, he finally resorts to a supernatural explanation of the origin of words: 'I think the truest account of these matters is this, Socrates, that some power greater than human laid down the first names for things, so that they must inevitably be the right ones.'

Similar conceptions may help when we come later to consider the conception of *logos* in Heraclitus, which seems so puzzlingly to be at the same time the word he utters, the truth which it contains, and the external reality which he conceives himself to be describing, and to which he gave the name of fire. The Pythagoreans, being a religious brotherhood as well as a philosophical school, show many traces of it. The earlier of them maintained that 'things were numbers'. To demonstrate it they said: 'Look! 1 is a point (·), 2 a line (·——·), 3 a surface (∴), and 4 a solid (∴̇). Thus you have solid bodies generated from numbers.' We may call this an unwarrantable and indeed incomprehensible leap from the abstract intellectual conceptions of mathematics to the solid realities of nature. The pyramid which they have made of the number 4 is not a pyramid of stone or wood, but non-material, a mere concept of the mind. Aristotle was already too far removed from their mentality to understand it, and complained that they 'made weightless entities the elements of entities which had weight'. But the anthropologist tells us again: 'Pre-logical mentality, which has no abstract concepts at command . . . does not distinctly separate the number from the objects numbered.' Numbers in fact, like everything else—whether objects or what we should distinguish from objects as mere conventional symbols, words or names—are endowed with magical properties and affinities of their own. Some knowledge of these facts should help us to approach these early Pythagoreans a little more sympathetically.

Before leaving this subject a warning must be uttered (strange as it may seem) against giving too much weight to what I have been saying. Pythagoras was not a primitive. The analogy with the primitive mind takes us a certain way and no further. He was a mathematical genius. He discovered among other things that the concordant notes in the musical octave correspond to fixed mathematical ratios, and what the ratios were. His mathematical bent had a profound influence on all his thought. Yet his unconscious assumptions were moulding it too, and the sort of considerations here put forward, if cautiously and critically applied to what we know of his doctrines, may help to let us into the secret of some of them. They must, however, be kept strictly in their place. The anthropological approach to the Greeks is so fascinating that it has led many a good scholar astray. It may be that magic and witchcraft were, as I have said, rife in Plato's time. It is equally important that he condemned them roundly. If what I have been saying leaves the impression that the Greek thinkers were a kind of superior medicine-men with a dash of rational thought thrown in, it will have been worse than useless. What it should do is to give some idea of the difficulties with which they had to contend, and so if anything heighten our appreciation of their achievements when we come to them. Moreover the history of Greek thought is in one of its aspects the process of emancipation from such popular preconceptions, many of which can be studied to-day among the peasants of modern Greece, and this in itself made some reference to them advisable as an introduction.

In making an historical study of the philosophy of a certain epoch, we must of course adopt a definition of the word which will apply to the thought of that time. Let us describe it therefore in a way which might not be agreed upon by all who call themselves philosophers to-day, but which is suitable in considering the philosophers of Greece. I myself should claim nevertheless, even though prepared for disagreement, that the divisions of its subject-matter which I shall adopt for our present purposes are as relevant to the intellectual problems of to-day as they were to those of the ancients.

It has two main sides, and as it reaches maturity develops a third.

1. *Speculative or scientific.* This is man's attempt to explain the universe in which he lives, the macrocosm. Nowadays the special sciences of nature have developed so far that they are distinguished from philosophy, and the latter term is reserved, in this aspect of it, for metaphysics. But we shall be speaking of a time when science and philosophy were both in their infancy and no line was drawn between them.

2. *Practical* (including ethical and political). The study of man himself, the microcosm, his nature and place in the world, his relations with his fellows. The motive for this is not usually, as with speculation about the nature of the universe, pure curiosity, but the practical one of finding out how human life and conduct can be improved.

Chronologically we shall find that in Greece the first appeared before the second, though here we must distinguish between casual reflections on human life and conduct, on the one hand, and moral philosophy on the other. 'Moral reflection, in consequence of the demands of life lived in common, preceded reflection about nature, whereas critical reflection on the principles of conduct, on account of these same demands, only begins late.' That remark of Henri Berr, in his preface to Robin's *Greek Thought*, was made with a general application. Apply it to Greece, and we see that the gnomic and didactic poetry of a Hesiod, Solon or Theognis—full of saws and aphorisms—precedes the beginnings of natural philosophy in Ionia in the sixth century. On the other hand, for anything that can be called a *philosophy* of human conduct—an attempt to base our actions on a systematic co-ordination of knowledge and theory—we must wait until the close of the fifth century. It comes with the Sophists and Socrates, when the first wave of enthusiasm over natural philosophy had spent itself, and the confidence of its adherents was being shaken by scepticism.

3. I said that as philosophy grows up it develops a third side. This is *critical philosophy*, including logic and epistemology or theory of knowledge. It is only

at a comparatively advanced stage of thought that people begin to ask themselves about the efficiency of the instruments with which they have been provided by nature for getting into touch with the world outside. What is our knowledge ultimately based on? Is it the evidence of the senses? We know that the senses may *sometimes* delude. Have we any proof that they ever bring us into contact with reality? Are our mental processes sound? We had better get to work on these processes themselves, analyse and test them, before we allow ourselves to think any more about the world outside. These are the questions that belong to critical philosophy. It takes thought itself for its subject-matter. It is philosophy become self-conscious. The way is paved for it as soon as a philosopher begins to doubt the evidence of the senses, as Heraclitus and Parmenides did in their different ways in Greece of the early fifth century. It did not make much progress until the later years of Plato, but it will be interesting as we go on to see the need for such a science gradually making itself felt.

Returning to the first two branches of philosophy —the metaphysical and the ethical—some philosophers will be equally interested in both and succeed in combining them in one single, integrated system. That was the aim of Plato, whose philosophic purpose was to combat two complementary tendencies of his age: (i) intellectual scepticism, which denied the possibility of knowledge on the ground that there were no lasting realities to be known: (ii) moral anarchy, the view that there were no permanent and universal standards of conduct, no higher criteria of action than what happened to seem best to a particular man at a particular moment. As a comprehensive solution to the double problem he offered his doctrine of Forms, to which we shall come in its due place.

More commonly, different thinkers are attracted to one or other of the two sides, as Socrates to the sphere of conduct or Anaxagoras to cosmic speculations. Usually also the whole thought of a particular age will incline more to one than to the other, for it depends in part at least on the state of society. Philosophers do not think in a void, and their results may be described as a product of

temperament × experience × previous philosophies.

In other words they are the reaction of a certain temperament to the external world as it presents itself to that particular man, influenced, in the case of most philosophers, by reflection on the remains of previous thinkers. And we may be sure that, just as no two men's temperaments are exactly alike, so no two men's external worlds—i.e. experience—are exactly alike.

That is why the answers to the ultimate questions of philosophy have been so widely different. Two men of contrasting temperament are bound to give different answers to philosophical questions. Indeed it is probable that the answers will not even be contradictory; they will simply be impossible to correlate at all. They will not only differ in content, they will be different *kinds* of answer. An example may make this clearer. Suppose two men are arguing about what the world is made of. One says it is all water, the other that it is all air. Then they are both answering the same question in the same way, and simply giving contradictory answers. They have a basis for argument, each may adduce facts of their common observation in support of his view, and there is a chance that one may end by convincing the other, But suppose the question—What after all *is* the world?—is being debated on a less crudely material, more philosophic level, and one man asserts that it is positive and negative charges of electricity, the other that it is a thought in the mind of God. It is unlikely that the two could spend a profitable hour of argument or make much progress together. They are different sorts of men. The second is probably quite ready to admit what the first says about electricity, but will not allow it to affect his answer. Similarly the first, though more likely to deny the truth of what the other says, will probably reply that it may or may not be true, but in any case is irrelevant.

The two answers belong to the two everlastingly opposed philosophical types, which betray themselves by their replies to what Aristotle called the eternal question: 'What is reality?' This is not such an impossible question as it sounds. It simply means: in considering anything, whether it be the whole Universe or a particular object in it, what do you regard as essential to it, which you would mention at once if asked the question 'What is it?' and what do you regard as secondary and unimportant? Anyone can easily find out to which of the two types he belongs. Suppose the question to be 'What is this desk?' and consider which of the two following answers appeals to you as the most immediately relevant: (a) wood, (b) something to put books and papers on. The two answers, it will be seen, are not contradictory. They are of different kinds. And the immediate and instinctive choice of one rather than the other shows one to be by temperament inclined to materialism or to teleology.

The two types may be clearly discerned among the ancient Greeks. Some defined things with reference to their matter, or as the Greeks also called it, 'the out-of-which'. Others saw the essential in purpose or function, with which they included form, for (as is pointed out e.g. by Plato in the *Cratylus*) structure subserves function and is dependent on it. The desk has the shape it has because of the purpose it has to serve. A shuttle is so shaped because it has to perform a certain function for the weaver. And so the primary opposition which presented itself to the Greek mind was that between matter and form, always with the notion of function included in that of form. And in answering the eternal question, the Ionian thinkers and later the atomists gave their reply in terms of matter, the Pythagoreans, Socrates, Plato and Aristotle in terms of form.

This division of philosophers into materialists and teleologists—matter-philosophers and form-philosophers—is perhaps the most fundamental that can be made in any age, our own included. Since, moreover, both sides are clearly and vigorously represented in the Greek tradition from the start, we shall do well to keep the distinction in the forefront of our minds.

CHAPTER II

MATTER AND FORM

(*Ionians and Pythagoreans*)

WE saw in the last chapter that philosophy as we shall be concerned with it has two main sides, dealing on the one hand with the nature and origins of the Universe at large and on the other with human life and conduct; and I warned any who might be primarily interested in ethical and political thought that when we go back to the beginnings of European philosophy in Greece it is speculation about the Universe that we shall encounter first. The whole period which we shall have under review is usually divided into two by the name of Socrates—with what justification we shall see as we proceed—and the characteristic mark of pre-Socratic thought is a consuming curiosity about the cosmos. The lifetime of Socrates saw a reaction against physical speculation and a shifting of philosophical interest to human affairs. Like all large generalizations, this is only approximately true. While in the Eastern part of the Greek world the Ionians were absorbed in the first attempts at a scientific explanation of the Universe, in the West the Pythagoreans were setting up the ideal of philosophy as a way of life, and the philosophic brotherhood as a kind of religious order; and the great successors of Socrates, Plato and Aristotle, while not neglecting the problems of human life, were both interested also in speculation about the world in which we live. For Plato indeed the human soul was at the centre; but in Aristotle the taste for the disinterested investigation of nature for its own sake reached its height. More than any other Greek did he possess the scientific temperament. Moreover the interest of the Pythagoreans in the human soul was rather religious and mystical than philosophical. We may say, however, that such an *exclusive* devotion to external nature as was exhibited by the Ionians became for ever impossible after the apparent breakdown of natural philosophy in the fifth century, and the importunate questionings of Socrates which brought human life into the very centre of the picture. How all this happened we shall now proceed to inquire.

European philosophy, in the sense of an attempt to solve the problems of the Universe by reason only, as opposed to the acceptance of purely magical or theological explanations, began in the prosperous commercial cities of Ionia, on the coast of Asia Minor, in the early sixth century B.C. It was, as Aristotle said, the product of an age already provided with the necessities for physical well-being and leisure, and its motive was simple curiosity. The Ionian or Milesian School is represented by the names of Thales, Anaximander and Anaximenes, and there is this much justification for calling it a school, that all three were natives of the same prosperous Ionian city of Miletus, their lifetimes overlapped, and tradition at least described their relations as those of master and pupil.

The object of their search may be described in two ways. They looked for something permanent, persisting through the chaos of apparent change; and they thought that they would find it by asking the question: 'What is the world made of?' The world as our senses perceive it seems restless and unstable. It exhibits continual and apparently haphazard change. Natural growth may proceed or may be thwarted by blind external forces. In any case it is followed by decay and nothing lasts for ever. Moreover we observe an apparently infinite plurality of unrelated objects. Philosophy started in the faith that beneath this apparent chaos there exists a hidden permanence and unity, discernible, if not by sense, then by the mind. This statement applies of course to all philosophy. As a modern writer on philosophical method has put it:

'There seems to be a deep-rooted tendency in the human mind to seek . . . something that persists through change. Consequently the desire for explanation seems to be satisfied only by the discovery that what appears to be new and different was there all the time. Hence the search for an *underlying* identity, a persistent stuff, a substance that is conserved in spite of qualitative changes and in terms of which these changes can be explained.'[1]

That description of the philosophic mind might have been written specially for the Milesians. They were already philosophers, and the basic problems of philosophy change little through the ages. Central is the faith that beneath the apparent multiplicity and confusion of the universe around us there exists a fundamental simplicity and stability which reason may discover.

Secondly, it seemed to the earliest speculators that this stability must be sought in the substance of which the world was made. This is not the only

[1] L. S. Stebbing, *A Modern Introduction to Logic*, (Methuen, 2nd ed. 1933), p. 404.

possible answer. It may equally be supposed that the material components of the world *are* in a constant flux of decay and renewal, *are* manifold and incomprehensible, but that the permanent and comprehensible element lies in its structure or form. If new matter as it comes along fits itself always to the same structure, it is the structure that we must try to understand. In Greece itself the champions of form against matter were to have their turn. At the beginning, however, the question asked was, in its simplest terms: 'What is the world made of?' Thales of Miletus said that it was water, or moisture, an answer which might open up all sorts of interesting possibilities, were it not that we know scarcely anything more about his views and can only conjecture what was the train of thought which led him to his conclusion. The most obvious explanation seems to be that water exhibits itself naturally to the senses, without any apparatus of scientific experiment such as was not then available, in the three forms solid, liquid and gaseous, as ice, water and steam. This is accordingly the explanation which occurs most readily to modern scholars, but it is interesting that Aristotle has a quite different suggestion. He, too, was guessing—whatever Thales may have written was already lost in his day—but he was at least a Greek and nearer to Thales than ourselves. I want to suggest some reasons why he may have been right, but this is a topic to which we had better return when we have looked at the views of the other two Milesians.

Beyond his statement that the underlying substance of the Universe is water, we know little of Thales's philosophical views. There are one or two aphorisms, difficult to interpret without a context, and several anecdotes. The story in Herodotus that he predicted a solar eclipse, which can be dated to the year 585 B.C., may be taken to be sufficiently *bien trouvé* to give us his approximate date. The prediction is by no means impossible with the aid of the Babylonian records of which he is said to have been a student. We know more of his younger fellow-citizen Anaximander, who left writings which were certainly available to Aristotle and Theophrastus, and the work of Theophrastus on the *Opinions of the Natural Philosophers* was the basis of the Graeco-Roman compilations which have come down to us.

The thought of Anaximander was already of some subtlety. He saw this present world as a warring concourse of opposite qualities, of which four were primary—hot and cold, wet and dry. The world-process is a cyclic one. The sun's heat dries up water, water puts out fire. On a world-scale it is observable in the cycle of the seasons, and though one or other of the opposites may prevail for a time, the balance is constantly being restored. Now since the essential thing about these qualities is their mutual opposition, it follows that the primary substance of the Universe cannot be characterized by any one of them—cannot, Anaximander would have said, *be* any one of them, for it is most unlikely that at this early stage of thought quality and substance were differentiated. Had Anaximander been asked whether, when he spoke as he did of 'the hot' or 'the cold', he meant a substance or a quality, he would probably not have understood the question. If then, as Thales had supposed, all were originally water, or 'the moist', there could never be heat or fire, since water does not generate fire, but destroys it. Hence he imagined the first state of matter to be an undifferentiated mass of enormous extent, in which the antagonistic elements or their properties were not yet distinct, though it contained them as it were in a latent or potential form, a complete fusion. He called it the *apeiron,* a word which means 'without boundaries', and in later Greek was used in two main senses: (*a*) not bounded externally, i.e. spatially infinite, and (*b*) without internal boundaries, i.e. in which no distinctions of separate component parts, or elements, could be observed. It is unlikely that Anaximander had arrived at the notion of strict spatial infinity, and although he certainly conceived his matrix to be of vast and indeterminate extent, the thought uppermost in his mind was probably the lack of internal distinctions, since this is the concept which would solve the problem that was obviously on his mind, that of the original condition of the opposites.

This primal mass was pictured by Anaximander as being in everlasting motion, as a result of which it happened, at some time in some part of it, that the opposite qualities, or substances containing them, began to separate themselves out. Hence arose what Anaximander called a seed or germ of a world, a fertile nucleus—for he borrowed that term from the realm of organic nature. At first it must have been something like the whirling nebulas known to modern astronomy. Gradually the cold and wet element condensed into a wet mass of earth at the centre, wrapped round in cloud or mist. The hot and dry showed itself as a sphere of flame enclosing the whole, which as it revolved burst apart into rings or wheels of fire around which surged the dark mist from within the sphere. This is his explanation of sun, moon, and stars, each of which is really a ring of fire right round the earth, though only visible to us at one point where there is a hole in the encircling vapours through which the fire streams like air through a puncture in a bicycle tyre. Under the influence of the fire at the circumference, parts of the earth were dried out and separated from the water that surrounded them. Life first arose during this process in the warm mud or slime, for the origin of life was in moisture acted upon by warmth. The first animals were therefore fishlike, and enclosed in prickly or scaly coverings. From these developed all land-animals, including man, who has evolved ultimately from a sort of fish.

The earth in this account is cylindrical like a drum, and rests unsupported at the centre of a spherical universe. Here Anaximander gave, to a question which had long puzzled the Greeks, an answer which for subtlety of thought was ahead of many of his successors. What did the earth rest on? If on water, as Thales had said, then what did the water rest on, and so forth? It rests on nothing, said Anaximander, and the reason it does not fall is simply that, being at the centre of a spherical universe, and hence equidistant from all its points, it could have no reason for falling in one direction rather than in another. It is in the position of the donkey placed exactly half-way between two bundles of hay, which dies of starvation because it cannot decide which way to turn.

This cosmogony of Anaximander's, in spite of certain fantastic elements, was a remarkable achievement for the dawn of rational thought. He made some use of observation, supporting his notion of the drying-out of the earth by the presence of fossilized shells in inland districts, and his argument that man had evolved from a lower form of life by the observation that, in his present state, man is helpless and dependent for a considerable time after birth. There must have been a time when the young were carried about for protection by the parent, and this, he observes, is done by certain species of large fish. To assess his quality, we must not only look back on him from our own time, but see him in relation to previous and contemporary Greece. His was an age when the supernatural was still taken for granted, when the forces of nature were attributed to the actions of anthropomorphic gods, a Zeus or a Poseidon, and the origin of the Universe had hitherto been sought in grotesque stories about a sexual union of heaven and earth, conceived as vast primeval deities, and their forcing-apart by another gigantic spirit. With Anaximander human reason asserted itself and produced what, right or wrong, was for the most part an account in purely natural terms of the origin of the world and life.

From Anaximenes, the remaining member of the Milesian School, we have no connected account of cosmogony, but a new claimant for the title of primary substance. This is air (Greek *aer*, which in ordinary speech—and there is no question at this stage of a technical scientific terminology—meant both air and mist or fog). In its natural, or what Anaximenes called its most evenly distributed state, it is the invisible atmosphere, but it is capable of being condensed into mist and water, and so, he claimed, still further into solid substances like earth and stones. When it becomes still rarer, it also becomes hotter and turns into fire. His chief interest seems to have lain in discovering a natural process by which it might be supposed that the changes in the primary substance take place, whereby our manifold world comes into being. Anaximander's word for the process which gave rise to our world had been 'separating-out', but it could fairly be said that this was no more than a brilliant conjecture which could not be verified in any known process of nature. For it Anaximenes substituted the observed fact of condensation and rarefaction, whereby we see air reduced to moisture and vice versa. To illustrate the connexion of rarefaction with heat and condensation with cold he pointed out that if we breathe with our lips nearly closed the breath emerges cold, whereas if we open our mouths to give it more room it is warmer.

One particular tenet of Anaximenes throws light on the outlook of the whole school. He said that in its purest and rarest form of all, the air which is the ultimate world-substance is also the stuff of life. A small portion of this soul-stuff, which properly belongs by its nature to the outermost reaches of the Universe beyond the adulterated atmosphere which we breathe, is imprisoned in the body of each animal or human being, and forms its soul. 'Our soul', said one of his followers, 'is air, hotter than the air outside us, though much colder than the air at the sun.' This man also expressed the same thing by saying that man's soul is 'a small part of the god', the god being the Universe, which we thus learn is still thought of by these men as being alive. For all their astonishing freedom from theological preconceptions, this one idea remained. It was indeed a legacy from pre-rational thought, for this material conception of the soul as air or breath is of course a primitive one to which anthropologists have found parallels among savage peoples all over the world, and it was certainly coupled among the earlier Greeks with the idea that the world as a whole was a living creature.

Nevertheless for these early scientists there was a special reason why it should still have seemed necessary. Besides the one question that they asked —What is the world made of?—there seems to us to be another which needs answering as well, namely: if the world is at bottom, and was originally, one substance, why did it not remain so, a dead, static mass of water or whatever it was? What was the motive cause which first started it changing? This question occurs to us because from recent science we have inherited the notion of matter as in itself something dead or inert, which needs to be called into motion by an outside force. Perhaps the distinction between matter and force is not so obvious in this century as it was in the last, nor does the natural scientist nowadays regard it as within his province to deal with the problem of a first cause. But philosophy cannot ignore it, and we are speaking of men to whom science and philosophy were one indivisible field of knowledge. How did they deal with this question of the cause of motion?

As Cornford put it, 'If we would understand the sixth-century philosophers, we must disabuse our minds of the atomistic conception of dead matter in mechanical motion and of the . . . dualism of matter and mind.' Aristotle, who was already criticizing the Ionians for (as it appeared to him) 'lazily shelving' the question of the motive cause, remarks in one place, without comment, that none of them made earth the primary substance. There was surely a good reason for this. They wanted a substance which would *explain its own movement*, as in those early days it was still possible to imagine it doing. One thought of the ceaseless tossing of the sea, another of the rushing of the wind, and on the threshold of rational thought the natural explanation of their apparently self-caused movement was that they were eternally alive. Thus we find that all of them, while in other respects avoiding the language of religion and completely discarding the anthropomorphism of their time, yet applied the name God or 'the divine' to their primary substance. So Anaximander called his *apeiron* and Anaximenes the air. Thales is credited with the dictum: 'Everything is full of gods', which Aristotle interpreted as meaning that 'soul is mingled in the whole'. The stuff of the world must be the stuff of life, and that is why I think there is more to be said for Aristotle's conjectures about the reason for Thales's choice of water than modern commentators are inclined to allow. His words are: 'He got the notion probably from seeing that the nutriment of all things is moist, and that heat itself is generated by the moist and kept alive by it . . . and that the semen of all creatures has a moist nature, and water is the origin of the nature of moist things.'

The lines of thought suggested by Aristotle are those which link up water with the idea of life: the moisture which is a necessary part of food and semen, and the fact that vital heat, the warmth of a living body, is always a damp warmth. (The connexion between heat and life, an obvious fact of experience, was insisted on by the Greeks as essential and causative more than it is to-day.) If that was Thales's idea, we find it explicitly paralleled by Anaximander who accounts for the origin of life by the action of heat on watery or slimy matter.

Seeing that these thinkers only asked their single question: 'What is the world made of?' it is tempting to label them materialists. This, however, would be misleading, since that term in ordinary modern speech stands for one who has made a choice between the known alternatives of matter and spirit as the ultimate causes of things, and consciously denies any originating power to the spiritual. What we must try to understand is a state of mind before matter and spirit had been distinguished, so that the matter which was the sole and unique fount of all existence was itself regarded as endowed with spirit or life. As philosophy progresses, it finds it more and more difficult to maintain this two-in-one conception, and not the least interesting aspect of the development of Greek thought is that which shows matter and spirit straining increasingly at the bonds which unite them. Matter has to be credited with more and more of the attributes of spirit, including mind, until the question comes to a head and a break is inevitable.

For the rest of this chapter let us turn to the Pythagoreans. The two main streams of tradition in early Greek thought were spoken of in later antiquity as the Ionian and the Italian. The latter begins with Pythagoras, who although an Eastern Greek by birth left his native island of Samos early in life and migrated to South Italy round about 530 B.C., where he settled and founded his brotherhood in the town of Croton. For political reasons they were persecuted and dispersed, and by the fifth century scattered Pythagorean communities were to be found in various parts of Greece. To say nothing about the Pythagorean tradition would be to give a very one-sided view of Greek philosophy and to omit something that was a potent influence on the mind of Plato. Yet it would perhaps defeat our present purpose to devote much space to them here, owing to the obscurity which envelops much of their doctrine and their history.

For this obscurity there are good reasons. Among the Pythagoreans, the motive for philosophy was not what it had been for the Ionians, simple scientific curiosity. They were a religious brotherhood, and this had certain consequences. Some at least of their doctrines were held to be secret, and not to be divulged to the profane. The founder himself was canonized, or regarded as semi-divine. This meant in the first place that a haze of miraculous legend gathered about him, from which it is difficult to disentangle the life and teaching of the historical Pythagoras. In the second place it was considered a pious duty to ascribe any new doctrine to the founder himself, and considering that the school had a long history, including a particularly flourishing revival among the Romans in the time of Cicero, it is obviously difficult to find out just what were Pythagoras's own beliefs or those of the school in its early days.

On its religious side, the core of Pythagoreanism was a belief in the immortality of the human soul, and its progress through a series of incarnations not only as man but also in the bodies of other creatures. With this is connected the most important of Pythagorean taboos, their abstention from animal flesh. For the beast or bird which you eat may haply be inhabited by the soul of your grandmother.

If that is so, if the transmigration of souls is possible and usual, then all life is akin, and the kinship of nature is another Pythagorean tenet. It went further than we might think, for the animate world extended further for them than it does for us. They believed indeed that the Universe as a whole was a living creature. In this they agreed with the Ionians, but they saw implications in it which were foreign to Anaximander or Anaximenes and came rather from mystical religious than from rational sources. The cosmos, they held, is surrounded with a boundless quantity of air or breath, which permeates and gives life to the whole. It is the same thing which gives life to individual living creatures. From this relic of popular belief, rationalized as we saw by Anaximenes, a religious lesson was now drawn. The breath or life of man and the breath or life of the infinite and divine Universe were essentially the same. The Universe was one, eternal and divine. Men were many and divided, and were mortal. But the essential part of man, his soul, was not mortal, and owed its immortality to this fact, that it was a fragment or spark of the divine soul, cut off and imprisoned in a mortal body.

Man had thus an aim in life, to shake off the taint of the body and, becoming pure spirit, rejoin the universal spirit to which he essentially belonged. Until the soul could purify itself completely, it must continue to undergo a series of transmigrations, exchanging one body for another. This meant the retention of individuality so long as the allotted cycle of births was incomplete, but there can be little doubt that the ultimate aim was the annihilation of self in reunion with the divine.

These beliefs the Pythagoreans shared with other mystical sects, notably with those who taught in the name of the mythical Orpheus. But the originality of Pythagoras is seen when we ask what are the means whereby the aim of purification and union with the divine may be attained. Hitherto purity had been sought by ritual, and the observance of mechanical taboos such as the avoidance of corpses. Pythagoras retained much of this, but added a way of his own, the way of the philosopher.

The doctrine of the kinship of nature, which may be said to be the first principle of Pythagoreanism, is a relic of ancient belief, having much in common with the notion of magical sympathy. Its second principle is something rational and typically Greek. That is, the emphasis laid by Pythagoras on form or structure as the proper object of study, together with an exaltation of the idea of *limit.* If, as a classical professor recently stated in his inaugural lecture, a characteristic mark of the Greeks is their preference for 'the intelligible, determinate, mensurable, as opposed to the fantastic, vague and shapeless', then Pythagoras was the foremost apostle of the Hellenic spirit. The Pythagoreans, as convinced moral dualists, drew up two columns under the headings of good things and bad things. In the good column, along with light, unity and the male, came limit; in the bad column, with darkness, plurality and the female, is placed the unlimited.

The religion of Pythagoras embodied, as we have seen, a kind of pantheism. The world is divine, it is therefore good, and is a single whole. If it is good, alive and a whole, that is because, said Pythagoras, it is *limited*, and displays an *order* in the relations of its various parts. Full and efficient life depends on organization. We see this in individual living creatures, which we call organisms to indicate that they have all their parts arranged and subordinated to the end of keeping the whole alive (Greek *organon* = tool or instrument). So with the world. The only sense in which it can be called a single whole, as well as good and living, is that it has fixed limits and is therefore capable of organization. The regularity of world-phenomena was thought to support this. Days succeed nights and seasons seasons in due and invariable order. The wheeling stars exhibit (as was thought) eternal and perfectly circular motion. In short the world may be called a *kosmos*, an untranslatable word which combined the notions of order, fitness, and beauty. Pythagoras is said to have been the first to call it by this name.

Pythagoras, being by nature a philosopher, argued that if we want to identify ourselves with the living cosmos, to which we believe ourselves to be essentially akin, then while not neglecting the old religious rules, we must first and foremost study its ways and find out what it is like. This in itself will bring us closer to it, as well as enabling us to conduct our lives in closer conformity to the principles which it reveals. Just as the Universe is a *kosmos*, or ordered whole, so Pythagoras believed that each one of us is a *kosmos* in miniature. We are organisms which reproduce the structural principles of the macrocosm.

And by studying these structural principles, we develop and encourage the elements of form and order in ourselves. The philosopher who studies the *kosmos* becomes *kosmios*—orderly—in his own soul.

Pythagoras's own interests were first and foremost mathematical. It may be taken as established that this does not mean simply a superstitious playing with numbers, but that he made real and considerable advances in mathematics. The discoveries which he made were totally and astonishingly new. If we do not realize how exciting and fresh they must have seemed, we shall not be in a state of mind to sympathize with the extraordinarily wide application which it seemed right to him to give them. We must allow for a remnant of primitive thinking too: we remember what has been said about the savage's irrational confusion between numbers and the objects numbered. But his own remarkable discoveries must have seemed to give irrefutable confirmation, on purely rational grounds, to these earlier ways of thought.

His most striking discovery, and the one which is said to have exercised the widest influence over his thought and to have been the foundation of his mathematical philosophy, was in the field of music. He found out that those intervals of the musical scale which are still (I believe) called the perfect consonances can be expressed arithmetically as ratios between the numbers 1, 2, 3 and 4. These are the numbers which, added together, make 10, and the number 10, in the curious Pythagorean combination of mathematics and mysticism, was called the perfect number. It was illustrated graphically by the figure called the *tetraktys*, i.e. ∴̇. The octave is produced by the ratio 2 : 1, the fifth 3 : 2, and the fourth 4 : 3. Now if one did not know this, it is not the sort of thing that would occur to one while playing the lyre, and perhaps picking out the notes with a certain amount of trial and error. The discovery lay in the existence of an *inherent* order, a numerical organization within the nature of sound itself, and it appeared as a kind of revelation concerning the nature of the Universe.

The general principle which it was taken to illustrate was that of the imposition of limit (*peras*) on the unlimited (*apeiron*) to make the limited (*peperasmenon*). This was the general Pythagorean formula for the making of the world and all that it contains, and it was coupled with the moral and aesthetic corollary that limit was good and the unlimited evil, so that the imposition of limit and the formation of a *kosmos*, which they claimed to see in the world as a whole, was evidence of the goodness and beauty of the world and an example to be followed by men. Owing to Pythagoras's discovery, music provided for his followers the best instance of this principle at work. Its suitability was enhanced by the *beauty* of music, to which Pythagoras like most Greeks was sensitive, for the word *kosmos* carried to a Greek the suggestion of beauty as well as order. It was thus further evidence for the equation of limit with goodness that its imposition on the field of sound brought beauty out of disharmony. The whole field of sound, then, ranging indefinitely in opposite directions—high and low—is an instance of the unlimited. Limit is represented by the numerical system of ratios between concordant notes which reduces the whole to order. It is marked out according to an intelligible plan. This plan is not imposed on it by man, but has been there all the time awaiting his discovery. In Cornford's words: 'The infinite variety of quality in sound is reduced to order by the exact and simple law of ratio in quantity. The system so defined still contains the unlimited element in the blank intervals between the notes; but the unlimited is no longer an orderless continuum: it is confined within an order, a *kosmos*, by the imposition of limit or measure.'

This process, grasped here in a single striking instance, the Pythagoreans supposed to be the ruling principle at work in the Universe as a whole. It is here that their cosmology differs essentially from the Ionian type, giving one the right to call it a philosophy of form and theirs a philosophy of matter. They spoke of a mixture of opposites and left it at that. The Pythagoreans added the notions of order, proportion, and measure, i.e. they laid the stress on *quantitative* differences. Each separate thing was what it was not because of its material elements (which were common to all), but because of the proportion in which those elements were mixed; and since it is in this element of proportion that one class of things differs from another, so they argued that this, the law of its structure, was the essential thing to discover if one wanted to understand it. The emphasis is shifted from the matter to the form. Structure is the essential thing, and this structure could be expressed numerically, in terms of quantity. Is it now surprising, considering the inchoate state of philosophy at the time, and the absence of any systematic study of logic or even of grammar, that they expressed their new-found conviction by saying that 'things were numbers'?

That gives their general line of thought, and we cannot here go into its many individual applications. One, however, may be mentioned as an illustration, and for the powerful influence which it exercised over a very important branch of Greek science, a branch of science in which Greek, and hence ultimately Pythagorean, ideas were still regarded as canonical throughout the Middle Ages and beyond, in the Moslem East as well as in the Christian West. That is, the study of medicine. Limit and order are good, and the well-being of the world and of every creature in it depends on a right mingling (*krasis*) of the elements of which it is composed. It is then in a state of *harmonia*, the word which (in Greek as in English) primarily applied to music being extended to cover the whole field of nature. To the microcosm this doctrine was applied in the theory that bodily health was dependent on the rightly proportioned mixture of the physical opposites: hot and cold, wet and dry. If they are in a state of *harmonia* in the body, then, as the doctor in Plato's *Symposium* puts it, the most mutually hostile elements in it are reconciled and taught to live in amity: 'and by the most hostile I mean the most sharply opposed, as hot to cold, bitter to sweet, dry to wet'. This dogma of the importance of maintaining—or restoring in the case of sickness—the right quantitative relationships between opposite qualities became the corner-stone of Greek medicine, which started in a Pythagorean atmosphere with the work of Alcmaeon of Croton.

Pythagorean notions have had such a long history

in philosophy and literature that other illustrations will easily suggest themselves. I cannot for example go into the doctrine of the harmony of the spheres, against whose appealing but fragile beauty the prosaic mind of Aristotle directed some of its heaviest logical batteries. But at least we have seen something of the field of thought in which such a strange idea was born, and have a glimpse of the world which lay behind the words of Lorenzo to Jessica as they rested on the moonlit bank outside the house of Portia:

> Sit, Jessica. Look how the floor of heaven
> Is thick inlaid with patines of bright gold.
> There's not the smallest orb which thou behold'st
> But in his motion like an angel sings,
> Still quiring to the young-eyed cherubins.
> Such harmony is in immortal souls;
> But whilst this muddy vesture of decay
> Doth grossly close it in, we cannot hear it.

CHAPTER III

THE PROBLEM OF MOTION

(*Heraclitus, Parmenides and the pluralists*)

THE next philosopher in the succession is the enigmatic Heraclitus, who earned even in antiquity the nicknames of 'The dark one' and 'The Riddler'. Although the exact dates of his life are unknown, his position in the history of philosophy is fixed well enough by the fact that he criticized Pythagoras by name and is himself fairly obviously alluded to by Parmenides. He must have been at work just about the turn of the sixth and fifth centuries B.C.

If we find him difficult to understand, this is not only because we possess no more than a few fragments of what he actually wrote. He had clearly a haughty and contemptuous mind, and delighted in throwing out isolated oracular sayings rather than developing a patient and continuous line of argument. His method of communication is like that of the Delphic oracle, which, he says, 'neither utters nor hides its meaning, but shows it by a sign'. Nevertheless it is worth trying to get at some of the ideas underlying his disjointed pronouncements. They reveal an interesting stage in the history of thought.

The target of his criticism in Pythagoras and others was their investigation into external nature, their search for facts. 'Polymathy—the learning of many things—does not teach understanding,' he wrote. 'Otherwise it would have taught Hesiod and Pythagoras, Xenophanes and Hecataeus.' Such learning is got through the senses, but 'Eyes and ears are bad witnesses if the soul is without understanding'. The senses show a different world to each man. Look within yourself—i.e. to your own mind—and you will discover the *logos* which is the truth, and is common to all things. It is the first explicit step in the undermining of the senses as guides to truth.

The hidden law of nature which he claimed to have discovered seems to have been that all things live by conflict, which is therefore essential to life and thus good. The Pythagorean ideal of a peaceful and harmonious world he rejected as an ideal of death. 'War is the father of all', he said, and 'Strife is justice'. This was probably aimed at Anaximander, who had described the continual encroachment of the opposites on one another as injustice, for which in turn they have to pay the penalty. Hitherto philosophers had sought for permanence and stability. There is none, said Heraclitus, nor should one desire a stagnant world. Whatever lives, lives by the destruction of something else. 'Fire lives the death of air, and air of fire; water lives the death of earth, earth that of water.' The Pythagoreans spoke of a harmony of opposites, but how can opposites be in harmony except unwillingly? It is only, he said, an attunement of opposite tensions, like that in a bow. We must picture, I take it, a bow ready strung but not in use. As it leans against the wall, one sees no movement, and thinks of it as a static object, completely at rest. But in fact a continuous tug-of-war is going on within it, as will become evident if the string perishes. The bow will immediately take advantage, snap it and leap to stretch itself. The basis of equilibrium is struggle, which is therefore good in itself, since it is the source of life. It is absurd to call one aspect or stage of it good and another bad.

'The world', said Heraclitus, 'is an ever-living fire, kindled in measures and in measures going out.' If we supposed him, like the Ionians, to have believed in a single primary stuff out of which the world had evolved, then fire would be his primary substance. But Heraclitus was not like the Ionians. He did not believe in a cosmogony like Anaximander, an evolution of the world out of a primary simple state. It 'is, was, and ever will be' what it is now, and fire provides rather a kind of symbol of its nature. It is the best material expression (and no other sort of expression was then possible) of his two central principles: (i) everything is born of strife, and (ii) everything is in constant flux. For fire in the first place only lives by consuming and destroying, and secondly it is constantly changing in its material, even though it may, like a candle-flame, look steady and permanent enough for a while. If the whole world lives like that, it is aptly described as a sort of fire.

Heraclitus's conception of the *logos* is curious and difficult. 'Listen not to me, but to the *logos*', he says, where *logos* seems to have one of its usual meanings of 'account' or 'description', yet is already given a kind of existence independent of its teller, so that the two can be contrasted. The *logos* is true for ever, all things come to pass in accordance with it, it is common to all, and 'one must follow what is common'. It is presumably identical with the 'thought' (*gnome*) by which, he says, 'all things are steered through all things'. A later commentator says that according to Heraclitus 'we draw in the divine logos by breathing', i.e. the divine mind that steers the universe is (*a*) identical with the mind in us, as with the Pythagoreans, (*b*) still something material. It is in fact the same as the cosmic fire, for according to another ancient expositor of Heraclitus, 'He says that this fire is intelligent, and is the cause of the arrangement of the whole.' The notion of rational fire shows how hard it is becoming to explain everything without advancing beyond the notion of the material.

Heraclitus spoke in riddles, said the Greeks, and there were two main reasons for this. First, his own temperament made him delight in spectacular and paradoxical language. He may give us straightforward paradox, like 'Good and evil are one', or again a fascinating but tantalizing image, such as: 'Time is a child playing draughts; the kingdom is a child's.' Secondly he is difficult because thought with him had reached a peculiarly difficult stage. He could no longer accept the simple Ionian cosmogonies, nor find it easy and natural to confine life and thought in the strait-jacket of material substance. They were clearly due to burst it very soon.

The break came about in a strange way. It was ultimately due to the work of a thinker both powerful and limited, whose power and limitations alike formed a watershed in Greek thought. This thinker was Parmenides, whose life fell in the first half of the fifth century. According to Plato's dialogue about him, he was sixty-five about the year 450. After him Greek philosophy could never be the same, for everyone, even Plato and Aristotle, felt that they had to take account of him and, as it were, lay his ghost.

He was the exact reverse of Heraclitus. For Heraclitus, movement and change were the only realities; for Parmenides, movement was impossible, and the whole of reality consisted of a single, motionless and unchanging substance. This extraordinary conclusion he reached by a train of thought no less extraordinary.

There is a sentence, the authorship of which I cannot remember, which has several times been set for comment in the Classical Tripos at Cambridge. It is to the effect that many problems in Greek philosophy resulted from a confusion of grammar, logic, and metaphysics. The three were confused because, as separate subjects of study, none of them could yet be said to exist; and this is something which it is particularly important to remember in trying to understand Parmenides. The ordinary tools of logic, and even of grammar, which we have inherited so that they are now part of the unconscious mental processes of the least philosophical of us, were not available to him. It requires an effort to think oneself back into the skin of such a pioneer.

One idea which the Greeks at this stage found it difficult to absorb was that a word might have more than one meaning. Their difficulty no doubt had something to do with the proximity of the primitive magical stage at which a word and its object formed a single unity. Now the verb 'to be' in Greek meant 'to exist'—like the English word in the Biblical sentence: 'Before Abraham was, I am.' Of course in ordinary speech it was used in its quite different sense of having a certain quality, as to be black, cold etc., but this was a difference to which no one had as yet devoted any conscious thought. In modern terms, the difference between the existential and the predicative use of the verb had not yet been elucidated. To Parmenides, the first to reflect consciously on the logic of words, it seemed that to say that a thing *is* could and should mean only that it exists, and this thought came to him with the force of a revelation about the nature of reality. His whole conception of the nature of reality springs from the attribution of this single, metaphysical force to the verb 'to be'. The Ionian philosophers had said that the world *was* one thing, but *became* many. But, said Parmenides, has this word 'become' any real meaning? How can a thing be said to change, as you say e.g. that air changed into water and fire? To change means 'to become what it is not', but to say of what is that it is not is simply untrue. What is cannot *not be* anything, for 'not to be' means to vanish out of existence. Then it would no longer be *what is*, but that is something which was assumed, and had to be assumed, from the beginning. The one and only initial postulate of Parmenides was that 'it is', i.e. one single thing exists. The rest followed.

It may sound like nonsensical playing with words, but it was taken very seriously at the time, and it was only Plato in his full maturity who, in the dialogue called *The Sophist,* cleared up the point that although they used the same word 'is', Parmenides and the people against whom he was arguing meant two different things. At the time his doctrine seemed unanswerable, and strange consequences followed. All change and movement were unreal, because they would involve *what is* becoming what it is not or where it is not, and to say of what is 'It is not' is nonsense. Movement was impossible for a second reason also, that there was no such thing as empty space. Space could only be described as 'where the real thing, that which is, was not'. But where you have not got that which is, you obviously only have that which is not, i.e. what does not exist.

The real world, then, all that is, must be a changeless, immovable mass of one kind of substance, and in eternal and changeless stillness it must always remain. One need hardly say that it does not appear to be that, but this did not daunt Parmenides. All that men imagine about the Universe, he said, all that they think they see and hear and feel, is pure illusion. Only the mind can reach the truth, and the mind—so he proclaimed with the simple arrogance of the first of all abstract thinkers—proves incontrovertibly that reality is utterly different.

The significance of Parmenides is that he started the Greeks on the path of abstract thought, set the mind working without reference to external facts, and exalted its results above those of sense-perception. In this the Greeks were apt pupils, so much so that according to some their genius for abstract thought and for neglecting the world of external fact set European science on the wrong track for a thousand years or so. Whether for good or evil, here we see the process at its beginning.

Some have classed Parmenides as a materialist, arguing that as he makes no distinction between the material and the non-material, his single unchanged reality must have been conceived as material. That particular question is unimportant and indeed unanswerable, seeing that we are still dealing with a period before the material and the non-material had been distinguished. What is important is that his reality was *non-sensible*, only to be reached by thought. To Plato the distinction between material and spiritual was plain. Yet he expresses it far more often by the words 'sensible' and 'intelligible'. Parmenides was the first to exalt the intelligible at the expense of the sensible, and consequently to call him—as he has been called—the father of materialism is about as misleading as it could be.

From now on, any philosophy which maintained that the manifold world had evolved from a primitive unity would no longer hold water. Parmenides had dealt a death-blow to material monism of the Ionian type. The first reaction was that the world of appearances must at all costs be saved. Men's common sense revolted and said that the familiar things which we can see and touch must be real. Since this could no longer be combined with a belief in a primal unity, they denied that part of Parmenides's premise which said that reality was substantially one. The immediately following philosophers are pluralists. Not until the greatest of all Greek thinkers, Plato, do we find one who agreed that no more than a quasi-existence could be ascribed to the changing world of rocks and plants and animals, and sought reality and unity alike in a world beyond space and time. And though Plato was much influenced by Parmenides, and wrote of him with the greatest respect, there were by that time many other influences as well that helped to mould his thought.

The pluralists are represented by Empedocles, Anaxagoras, and the atomic philosophy of Democritus. Empedocles is an intriguing figure, a combination of philosopher, religious mystic on Pythagorean lines, and magician or wonder-worker. The Western Greek world, the home of Pythagoreanism, tended to produce such combinations, and Empedocles's home was at Acragas in Sicily. No other age or country could have thrown up such a phenomenon. He claims that his knowledge is the key to power over the forces of nature, that by it men can arrest the winds, make rain, and even bring back the dead from Hades. He was a firm believer in the transmigration of souls. All this was an essential part of him and cannot be separated from his philosophy, which yet was a serious contribution to thought and the first attempt to escape the logical net of Parmenides, whose pupil he is said to have been.

Since the ultimate unity of matter must be given up if the phenomena are to be accounted for, Empedocles stated that all the four elements (his word for them means 'roots')—i.e. earth, water, air and fire—were real and ultimate. The world of phenomena he explained as consisting of a variety of combinations of these four root-substances in varying proportions. Like a true Pythagorean he laid great stress on proportion as a determining factor, and was even prepared to say—though on what grounds it is difficult to imagine—what the proportions were in some particular cases. Bone for example he declared to be composed of two parts of earth, two of water and four of fire. On this line of thought there is no need to assume the change—the actual coming-into-being or destruction—of anything real. The only 'realities' are the four root-substances, and they have existed from all time and always will exist. Natural creatures are not 'real', but only chance combinations of these elements. Motion of course there must be, and this he apparently thought could take place without the assumption of empty space, which Parmenides seemed to have proved to be non-existent. He imagined it as the motion of a fish through water, where as it progresses the water immediately closes round it and is always in contact with it at all points.

After Parmenides, the naive Ionian notion of material substance which moved itself as a living thing seemed no longer tenable, and it became necessary to posit a separate motive cause. Empedocles posited two, which he named Love and Strife. In his physical work, they appear as natural forces exercising a purely physical attraction and repulsion. Strife, by whose influence each element tends to dissociate itself from the others, is at the same time a tendency of like to like, whereby every particle seeks to attach itself to others of the same element. Love is the force which mingles one element with another to create composite creatures. Now the one, now the other gains the upper hand in turn, and the evolution of worlds is a circular process. When Love is supreme, the elements are fused together in a mass. When Strife has the victory, they exist in separate concentric layers—for the whole is conceived as spherical—with earth at the centre and fire at the circumference. A world like our own exists in the intermediate stages, exhibiting as it does great masses of earth drawn apart into continents and of water collected as seas, and at the same time all sorts of combinations of different elements which are such things as plants and animals. While capable of speaking of these forces like a physicist, Empedocles obviously regarded them as also possessing the psychological and moral character which was associated with their names. Here the religious teacher comes in. Love is that which brings the sexes together, and which causes men to think kindly thoughts and do good deeds. Strife on the other hand brings hurt and sin into the world. Stranger still, we have not even yet reached the stage at which such forces can be thought of as non-material. The conception simply did not exist. One would have thought that when motive causes had been separated from the matter moved, the trick was done. But the language of Empedocles shows that it was not so. Love is 'equal in length and breadth' to the world. She and Strife 'run through all things', like a kind of quicksilver.

In general, it is obviously necessary to deal with these systems in the barest outline. We cannot for instance go into Empedocles's explanation of the mechanism of sensation, interesting though it is. But it is tempting to mention one of the stranger results of Empedocles's system on account of its intrinsic interest, namely that when he came to details it involved him, as it were by accident (for there was no question of scientific observation), in an almost Darwinian theory of natural selection. He is a natural philosopher in this, that in his world there is no creative god, no mind adapting organisms to a purpose. Living creatures, like other natural bodies, have originated in purely chance combinations of the elements. He had to explain therefore why their structure and organs simulated so well the appearance of purpose. Eyes and ears, feet and hands, digestive organs and so forth seem so admirably adapted for the functions which they have to perform that it is difficult not to believe that they were designed with these in view. But, said Empedocles, it was not always so. Originally there must have been the strangest creatures—men with the heads of cattle, animals with branches like trees instead of limbs. But in the struggle for existence those less fitted for survival perished, and only those whose members happened to have come together in practical ways have survived.

With Anaxagoras we return to the Ionian tradition; not of course to naive monism, but to the tradition of philosophy as a scientific activity pursued from motives of curiosity, not mixed up in the curious Pythagorean way with mystical religious ideas. He came from Clazomenae near Smyrna, from the cradle of rational thought, and lived in Athens, where he was a member of the enlightened and sceptical circle which gathered around Pericles and Aspasia in the middle of the fifth century. He was in fact prosecuted for impiety and forced to leave the city. The motive was doubtless political, and aimed at him as a friend of Pericles, but the charge is interesting nevertheless. He was indicted for saying that the sun was not a divinity, but only a white-hot stone rather larger than the Peloponnese.

He evolved a highly complicated theory of the nature of matter, into which it is unnecessary to venture here. Not only is his exact meaning still a subject of dispute among the learned, so that it would be extremely difficult to explain it at all clearly without taking a long time about it, but it was not in itself a theory with which philosophy could rest content. It was a kind of half-way house, and interesting chiefly as pointing the way to the thorough-going atomic theory which followed it. The important thing for us to notice here is that with him for the first time a clear distinction was explicitly drawn between matter and mind. He boldly said, not only, like Empedocles, that there must be a moving cause apart from the matter which was moved, but that whatever was not matter must be mind.[1] Mind rules the world and has brought order into it out of confusion. We may notice by the way that no Greek ever spoke of creation in an absolute sense, of a god who brought something out of nothing. The creation of a world is always the imposition of order—*kosmos*—on an already existing chaos of matter.

With the conception of a mind behind the Universe, which governs and orders its changes, we seem to be getting back to a theistic outlook, but this time by the path of rational thought, not by a mere acquiescence in religious tradition. How far Anaxagoras was from that may be judged not only from his prosecution by the State as an atheist, but also from the opinion of Socrates and Plato. These philosophers, themselves passionate believers in the

[1] Some have seen the shreds of a materialistic conception still clinging in one or two of the epithets applied to mind by Anaxagoras, e.g. *katharos* ('pure'), *leptos* ('thin', 'fine', 'small', applied to finely ground grain or to fine and light materials). In reply to this it is surely pertinent to ask what other epithets were available to the poor man? It is a clear case of thought having outrun the resources of language. No one would accuse Plato of a materialistic outlook, yet he too speaks of 'thinking finely', using the adverb from *leptos*. A moment's reflection would show that our own speech is still full of such metaphorical uses of terms properly applying to physical objects. They are, and will remain, indispensable.

rational government of the Universe, censured him because, they declared, although he starts out by saying that mind is the ultimate cause of everything, he makes no use of this assumption unless he is at a loss to explain something in any other way. Then he 'drags in' mind, but otherwise he tries to explain everything like an atheistical scientist by physical, material causes. We must not therefore make too much of the novel doctrine of Anaxagoras, which was clearly not put forward in a way that offered any possibilities of development on the spiritual side. We get a consistent picture of his character, exemplified in the story of the soothsayer, who, when a ram with one horn was given to Pericles, interpreted the phenomenon as meaning that of the two political rivals—Pericles and Thucydides—the one who possessed the ram would be victorious. Anaxagoras however had the animal's skull dissected and demonstrated the natural cause of the abnormality, that its brain did not fill the cavity as usual, but was small and egg-shaped and connected with the root of the single horn. Plutarch adds that the people admired Anaxagoras much, but the soothsayer still more when Thucydides was ostracized.

The atomic theory is jointly attributed to Leucippus and Democritus, but the former is a shadowy figure, whose very existence was doubted by their great follower Epicurus and has been denied by some modern scholars. Of Democritus and his writings we know much more. He was a northern Greek, from Abdera in Thrace, and was born about 460 B.C., a younger contemporary of Anaxagoras. His works do not seem to have been well known at Athens, but his fellow-northerner

Aristotle admired him greatly and has much to say about him.

Atomism of course gains a special interest from its anticipation of modern views. It is hardly an exaggeration to say that the theory of Democritus remained in essentials unchanged until the nineteenth century. It is nevertheless important to remember the complete absence in classical Greece of the apparatus of scientific experiment which has led to the discoveries of modern times, and enabled each one to be tested. Why the Greeks, for all their brilliance of intellect, made at this time so little use of experimental methods, and no progress at all in the invention of apparatus for controlled experiment, is a complicated question. Aristocratic tradition and the presence of slaves no doubt had something to do with it, but are scarcely in themselves a sufficient explanation. To some small extent those in the Ionian succession made use of observation, but only spasmodically until the time of Aristotle, and of controlled experiment they had no idea. Their legacy lies elsewhere, in their astonishing powers of deductive reasoning.

As with everyone else at that period, the thinking of the atomists was carried out with one eye on the tiresome logic of Parmenides and his successors in the Eleatic school, as it was called, even if it was only to deny a part of what they had said. Always they were conscious of his shadow in the background. Their basic idea, like those of Empedocles and Anaxagoras, arose directly out of his contention that there could be no coming-into-being or destruction of anything real. Consequently the apparent birth and perishing of natural objects must be explained, as

Empedocles had also said, by regarding them as no more than chance combinations of a multiplicity of elements which alone can be supposed to deserve the name of existents. To explain them thus, they hit upon the truly brilliant conjecture (for as such it must be described) that the elements, or only true realities, were tiny solid bodies, far too small to be perceived by our senses, clashing and recoiling in endless motion through a boundless space. These *atomoi*—ironically enough, as it seems to-day, the word means 'unsplittable'—were the smallest extant particles of matter, solid, hard and indestructible. They were substantially identical, and differed in size and shape only. These properties alone, together with differences in their relative positions, motions, and distances from each other, were sufficient to account for all the differences of which our senses make us aware in perceptible objects. What we feel as hard has its atoms closely packed. Soft things are made of atoms wider apart, they contain more empty space and so are capable of compression and offer less resistance to the touch. The other senses are explained on the same lines. In taste, sweet things are made of smooth atoms, whereas harsh or bitter flavours are caused by hooked or sharp-pointed atoms which tear their way into the body making minute excoriations on the tongue. As late as 1675, we find this notion persisting. A French chemist, Lémery, wrote at that date[1]: 'The hidden nature of a thing cannot be better explained than by attributing to its parts shapes corresponding to all the effects it produces. No one will deny that the acidity of a liquid consists in pointed particles.

[1] Quoted by Cornford, *Before and After Socrates*, p. 26.

All experience confirms this. You have only to taste it to feel a pricking of the tongue like that caused by some material cut into very fine points.'

Colours were explained by the various positions of the atoms forming the surface of objects, which caused them to throw back or reflect in different ways the light which falls upon them, and which is itself of course a corporeal thing made of particularly small fine atoms moving quickly because of their smallness and roundness. The finest and most perfectly spherical, and hence the most mobile and volatile, of all the atoms form the souls of animals and men; so thoroughgoing was the materialism of Democritus.

Thus all substance is reduced to material substance, and all sensation ultimately to the sensation of touch. Even sight is explained in this way, by the curious and not very satisfactory supposition that objects are constantly throwing off from their surfaces fine films or skins of atoms which retain more or less the shape of the object as they drift through the air all the way to the eye. Thus although sight is a matter of direct contact between atoms and atoms, it is possible to be deceived about the nature of an object seen at a distance, because the material image which passes from it to the eye may become distorted or damaged on the way. The mechanics of sensation were pursued into considerable detail, and an extraordinary ingenuity was shown in trying to explain all its varieties without recourse to any other hypothesis than that of direct material contact.

One thing of course was a fundamental necessity to the atomic world-view. There must be empty space for the atoms to move about in. The hallmark of Democritus's thought, as Aristotle noted approvingly, was a determination to account for apparent fact and not be led astray by abstract argument. Hence he said that Parmenides's denial of the existence of void could not be upheld. It was contrary to common sense. Aware however that he was flying in the face of that great authority, he made his denial with a kind of schoolboy daring, for according to Aristotle he put it in the form: 'What is not does exist, no less than what is.' If material atoms were the only real substance, then empty space was not real in the same sense. Dimly aware that there must be some way out, the atomists did not yet command a language capable of such a phrase as 'not in the same sense', and paradox was their only resource.

They seem to have thought that, given infinite empty space with an infinite number of microscopic bodies loose in it, the bodies would inevitably move, and move aimlessly in any direction. This would naturally lead to collisions, and these to entanglements and combinations, since the atoms were of all sorts of shapes, including hooked and branched. Thus agglomerations of perceptible size were gradually built up, and a world began.

When Epicurus took up and developed the theory nearly two centuries later, he imagined the atoms as moving in the first place straight downwards because of gravity, or as he expressed it, by reason of their weight. He realized however—and it is a remarkable illustration of the acuteness of the Greek mind—that all bodies, though varying in size and hence, if they were solid atoms, in weight, would fall through a vacuum at a uniform speed. This is a point which was only re-established with some difficulty in the sixteenth century. Epicurus therefore had to think of something else to account for the first collisions. Hence he assumed that at some indeterminate point of time and space, and for no ascertainable reason, an atom was liable to make a tiny imperceptible swerve from its straight downward path. This deviation from the strict determinism which was of the essence of the original atomic theory had a curious sequel in that it was held to allow for free-will in a universe where otherwise man like everything else would have had to be regarded as entirely subject to a blind and inexorable destiny. Scientifically speaking it was a retrograde step, and Democritus was thinking more clearly when he saw that in infinite space the conception of *up* or *down* had no meaning, and there could be no reason for the atoms to move in one direction rather than another.

The atomists posited no separate moving cause like the attractive and repulsive forces of Empedocles or the Mind of Anaxagoras. Aristotle accused them of 'lazily shelving' the question of the origin of motion. But if one realizes—and it is not a very easy thing to do—what a bold and novel step it was, after what had seemed the inescapable arguments of Parmenides, to assert positively and definitely the existence of void, one can see how this itself might seem to them a sufficient answer to the problem. Parmenides had actually said that the reason why motion was impossible was that there was no space for things to move in. With this restriction removed, and the atoms let loose, as it were, in the vast emptiness, it might well have seemed as pertinent to ask

'Why should they stand still?' as 'Why should they move about?' The illustration which the atomists used, as a visible example of a kind of motion similar to that of the atoms, was the sort of thing one sees when a narrow shaft of sunlight is allowed to penetrate into a darkened room by a hole or crack in a shutter. The motes which appear in the sunbeam executing a continuous dance in all directions are not of course atoms, which are far below the level of visibility, but the motion of the atoms themselves must, they said, be imagined as similar.

CHAPTER IV

THE REACTION TOWARDS HUMANISM

(*The Sophists and Socrates*)

WE have now reached the second half of the fifth century B.C. Socrates is in middle life, Plato is born or about to be born. (He was born in 427.) It is the time when the reaction against physical speculation set in and philosophers began to direct their thoughts towards human life, the second of the two divisions of philosophy that I mentioned at the beginning. One reason for the change is not far to seek. It was a revolt of common sense against the remoteness and incomprehensibility of the world as the physicists presented it. The ordinary man was confronted with the choice of believing with Parmenides that all motion was illusion and reality an immovable plenum, or else 'saving the phenomena' (as the others had the impudence to call it) by accepting as the only realities atoms—invisible, colourless, scentless, soundless atoms—and void. Neither picture was either comforting or particularly credible. At any rate, if the physicists were to be believed, then what they called the *physis* or real nature of things was something utterly remote from the world in which we seem to live. If they were right, then the nature of the real world turned out to be of very little consequence to man, who had to deal every day with a world which was quite different.

To understand this attitude, we must of course remind ourselves again of the complete absence of any experimental proof of their assertions, and also of any form of applied science. The physicist of to-day tells me equally that the desk which seems so solid under my typewriter is in fact a whirling maelstrom containing more empty space than solid matter. I may retort that I do not experience it in that way, yet I cannot turn my back on him or conclude that his view of reality is therefore of no consequence to me. We are all only too dismally aware of the practical impact which atomic science may have upon our lives. The Greek was luckier. He could and did turn his back, and it is partly at least to this circumstance that we owe some of the most profound reflections on the nature and purpose of human life.

The reasons for the change were bound to be complex. Athens had become the acknowledged leader of Greece in intellectual as in other matters, so that thinkers from other parts of the Greek world, like Anaxagoras or Protagoras, tended to be attracted into her orbit and to make their homes there. But Athens from the year 431 was engaged in the long and terrible war which was to lead to her downfall thirty years later, and soon after its outbreak suffered all the horrors of the plague. If disinterested scientific inquiry demands, as Aristotle rightly said, at least a minimum of leisure and comfortable material circumstances, then Athens was no longer the place in which it was easy, but rather a city where the problems of human life and conduct were obtruding themselves more and more. Moreover, Athens was a democracy, a democracy small enough to ensure that the participation of all free citizens in her political life was a reality and not merely a question of voting for a political representative every few years. Some offices were filled by lot, and every citizen could feel that he had a good chance of playing an active part in the conduct of the state's affairs. This again fostered an ambition to learn more about the principles underlying political life and the arts which would ensure success in it.

Here however there is no room to be anything but strictly selective, so after that brief reminder that important social and political factors were at work as well, I propose to concentrate on the more philosophical reasons for the change, thus ensuring at least the advantage of a more continuous thread of argument to follow. The reaction away from the investigation of *physis* is sometimes attributed among other things to what has been called the bankruptcy of physical science, and we have already had a hint of what that phrase means. The basis of physical science in Greece, as we said at the beginning, was the search for permanence or stability, and for an underlying unity, in a universe superficially mutable and unstable, and consisting only of a most confusing plurality. To the ordinary man it must have seemed that the physicists had failed conspicuously. They offered him the choice between Parmenides and the atomists. Either he could accept unity in the world at the price of renouncing belief in everything that seemed to him real and admitting that all his sensations were false; or he could follow those who had given up all idea of a one behind the many and produced a world of nothing but infinite plurality; and not even they would allow the name of reality to the secondary qualities which made up most of the world of his experience, the world that could be seen and heard and smelt and tasted.

The reaction towards humanism is associated with the rise of a new class, the Sophists. It is often pointed out that the Sophists were not a particular philosophical school, but rather a profession. They were itinerant teachers, who made a living out of the new hunger for guidance in practical affairs which arose at this time from the causes I have mentioned: the increasing opportunities of taking part in practical politics, the growing impatience with the natural philosophers, and (one may add) an increasing scepticism about the validity of traditional religious teaching with its crudely anthropomorphic pictures of the gods. The word *sophistes* ('practitioner of wisdom') had not hitherto carried any derogatory implication. It was in fact the word applied to the seven sages of tradition. It was the unpopularity of the fifth-century Sophists which gave it the colouring that it has borne ever since.

Yet though one cannot call them a particular philosophical school, they had certain definite points in common. One was the essentially practical nature of their teaching, which they described as the inculcation of *arete*. We have already discussed the meaning of this word, whose practical import is illustrated by the story of the Sophist Hippias, who, as a sort of living advertisement of his powers, appeared at the Olympic Games wearing nothing which he had not made himself, down to the ring on his finger.

Secondly, the Sophists shared something which may more properly be called a philosophical attitude, namely a common scepticism, a mistrust of the possibility of absolute knowledge. This was a natural result of the impasse to which, it seemed, natural philosophy had come. Knowledge depends on two things: the possession of faculties capable of bringing us into touch with reality, and the existence of a stable reality to be known. As instruments of knowledge, the senses had now been severely treated, and so far nothing had been put in their place; and faith in the unity and stability of the Universe had been undermined, without, as yet, the emergence of the idea that there might be a permanent and knowable reality outside and beyond the physical world.

The lifeblood of philosophy is controversy. Once its first beginnings are past, any new development usually represents a reaction from previous thought. This is true of the greatest of the Greeks—Socrates, Plato and Aristotle. That is why it is worth spending some time, as we are doing, on their immediate predecessors in order to understand the springs of their own thought, and for the same purpose it is particularly important to grasp the point that we have come to now, that moral and political philosophy first arose in Greece (which means that it first arose in Europe) in an atmosphere of scepticism. It was this scepticism which Socrates and his successors made it their life-work to combat. In the physical field Democritus had said that the sensations of sweet and bitter, hot and cold, were only conventional terms. They did not correspond to anything real. For this reason what seemed sweet to me might seem bitter to you, or to myself if I were unwell, and the same water might seem warm to one of my hands and cold to the other. It was all a matter of the temporary arrangement of the atoms in our bodies and their reaction to the equally temporary combination in the so-called sensible object. The transference to the field of morals was only too easy, and was first made about this time, indeed, if later tradition is to be trusted, by an Athenian named Archelaus, a pupil of Anaxagoras. If hot and cold, sweet and bitter, have no existence in nature but are simply a matter of how we feel at the time, then, it was argued, must we not suppose that justice and injustice, right and wrong, have an equally subjective and unreal existence? There can be in nature no absolute principles governing the relations between man and man. It is all a question of how you look at it.

The sceptical standpoint of the Sophists may be illustrated by quotations from the two best-known and most influential of their number, Gorgias and Protagoras. The favourite title for a natural philosopher to give to his work had been 'On Nature (*physis*) or the Existent'. In deliberate parody of the many works with this title, Gorgias wrote a book to which he gave the name 'On Nature, or the Non-existent', and in it he set out to prove three things: (a) that nothing exists; (b) that if anything did exist, we could not know it; (c) that if we could know anything, we could not communicate it to our neighbour.

Protagoras expressed his views on religion thus: 'Concerning the gods, I have no means of knowing whether they exist or not, nor of what form they are; for there are many obstacles to such knowledge, including the obscurity of the subject and the shortness of human life.' He was also the author of the famous dictum: 'Man is the measure of all things', the meaning of which was—if we may trust Plato's interpretation—that the way things appear to one man is the truth for him, and the way they appear to another is the truth for him. Neither can convict the other of error, for if one sees things in one way, then that is the way they *are* for him, though they may be different for his neighbour. Truth is purely relative. Protagoras, however, allowed room for conventional views of truth and morals by adding that although no one opinion is *truer* than another, one opinion may be *better* than another. If to the eye of a man with jaundice all things appear yellow, they really are yellow for him, and no man has the right to tell him they are not. But it is worth while for a doctor to change that man's world by altering the state of his body so that things will cease to be yellow for him. Similarly if any man sincerely believes that it is good to steal, then that statement is true for him so long as he believes it. But the great majority for whom it both seems and is bad, ought to endeavour to change the state of his mind and lead it to beliefs which are not indeed truer, but better. The test by truth or falsehood is abandoned, and replaced by the pragmatic test.

The irreverent scepticism of the Sophists affected the hitherto unchallenged sanction of law, which was based on a belief in its divine origin. The earliest makers of constitutions, like Lycurgus the legendary founder of Sparta, were believed to have been inspired by Apollo, and it was still customary for law-givers to apply to his oracle at Delphi and obtain, if not its advice, at least its sanction for their own plans. This religious foundation for law was now being undermined not only by the atheistical trend of natural philosophy, which the Sophists took up with such zest, but also by external circumstances such as the increasing contact of the Greeks with foreign countries and the great body of contemporary law-making connected with the foundation of colonies. The Sophists were the children of their age. The first taught them the fundamental differences which might exist between the laws and customs of peoples living in different climes. As for the second, it was difficult to believe that constitutions came from heaven when one's own friends (or still worse, one's political enemies) were on the commission which drew them up. Protagoras himself was on the commission sent out in 443 B.C. to draft a constitution for the new Athenian colony of Thurii in South Italy. It is not surprising that he became the first promulgator of that theory of the origin of law which we now know as the social contract. He said that for their own protection from wild creatures and for the advancement of their standard of living men had at an early stage been obliged to band themselves together into communities. Hitherto they had had neither moral standards nor laws, but life in societies was found to be impossible if the standards of the jungle prevailed, and so, by slow and painful degrees, they learned the necessity of laws and conventions whereby the stronger pledge themselves not to attack and rob the weak simply because they *are* the stronger.[1]

[1] I am assuming that the myth told by Protagoras in Plato's dialogue of that name is truly mythical in the sense that the divine apparatus can be stripped away without any loss to the serious message which he intends to convey. No significance is to be attached to the fact that conscience and a sense of justice are there said to have been implanted in men at the orders of Zeus. This is perhaps not universally agreed, but not only is the mythical nature of the exposition insisted upon (and reflected in the fairy-tale beginning: 'Once upon a time'), but any other interpretation would be inconsistent with Protagoras's views on religion as stated elsewhere.

Given this initial premise, that laws and moral codes were not divine in origin but man-made and imperfect, it was possible to draw widely differing practical conclusions. Protagoras himself said that they had come into being because they were necessary. He championed the social contract therefore and urged submission to the laws. Other more radical Sophists repudiated it, and maintained the natural right of the stronger to have his way. Different conclusions might be drawn, but the premise was the same for all. All alike took their stand on the complete absence of absolute values and standards, whether based on theological considerations or not. All human action was regarded by the Sophists as based on experience alone and dictated by nothing but expediency. Right and wrong, wisdom, justice and goodness, were nothing but names, even though it might be argued that it was sometimes prudent to act as if they were more.

Into this world of thought came SOCRATES. This is the outlook which seemed to him at once intellectually mistaken and morally harmful, and which he made it his life-work to combat.[1]

Socrates is probably best known for the famous dictum which is usually translated 'Virtue is knowledge', and to find out what this means makes as good an approach as any to the centre of his teaching. It is best understood historically, that is, by relating it to the problems which previous and contemporary thought, and the circumstances of his

[1] For an understanding of Socrates, the excellent article of Professor R. Hackforth in *Philosophy*, vol. VIII (1933) is especially to be recommended.

time, had forced on his attention, and which he was doing his best to solve.

We know now that the word 'virtue' attaches false associations to the Greek *arete*, which meant primarily efficiency at a particular task. We have also seen that the opponents against whom Socrates's teaching was aimed claimed two things: (a) that they themselves could teach or impart *arete*, (b) that knowledge, at least knowledge which could be shared, was a chimera. There was no such thing. By equating *arete* with knowledge, therefore, Socrates's statement takes on the aspect of a deliberate challenge, which we can only recapture by thinking ourselves back to the times in which he lived.

One of the things about Socrates which irritated the sensible, practical Athenian was that he would insist on turning the talk to such humble and apparently irrelevant people as shoemakers and carpenters, when what they wanted to learn about was what constituted political ability or whether there was such a thing as moral obligation. If you want to be a good shoemaker, he said, the first thing necessary is to know what a shoe is and what it is meant for. It is no use trying to decide on the best sort of tools and material to use and the best methods of using them unless you have first formed in your mind a clear and detailed idea of what it is you are setting out to produce and what function it will have to perform. To use the Greek word, the *arete* of a shoemaker depended first and foremost on the possession of this knowledge. He ought to be able to describe in clear terms the nature of the thing he intended to make, and his definition should include a statement of the use to which it was to be put.

It was quite natural to speak of the *arete* of a shoemaker, just as one could also speak of the *arete* of a general or statesman. In no such case did the word have any necessary connexion with the moral aspect of their activities as our word 'virtue' would suggest. It meant that in them which made them good at their particular job, and by taking first the humble examples of the useful crafts, it was not difficult for Socrates to show that in each case the acquisition of this capacity depended on knowledge and that the first and most necessary knowledge was knowledge in each case of the end in view—what the man was setting out to do. Given a proper understanding of the end, the understanding of the means to be adopted could follow, but not otherwise. In every instance, therefore, *arete* depended first on having a definite job to do, and secondly on a thorough knowledge of what the job was and what it aimed at effecting. If then (he proceeded) there is any legitimate sense in which we can talk about *arete* unqualified, as the Sophists were professing to teach it—that is, efficiency in living for any man as such—it follows that there must be an end or function which all alike, as human beings, have to perform. The first task therefore, if we are to acquire this universal human virtue, is to discover what the function of man is.

Now I would not say that from the records of Socrates's teaching which we have in the writings of his pupils (for he himself wrote nothing, believing that the only thing of value was the living interchange of ideas by question and answer between two people in personal contact) we find the answer to this primary question of the universal end or aim of human life. Its absence from his teaching was, I should say, one reason which made the more positive Plato feel it his duty not only to reproduce his master's teaching but to carry it a stage further. It is in keeping with Socrates's character that the answer should not be there. He was accustomed to say that he did not himself know anything, and that the only way in which he was wiser than other men was that he was conscious of his own ignorance, while they were not. The essence of the Socratic method is to convince the interlocutor that whereas he thought he knew something, in fact he does not. The conviction of ignorance is a necessary first step to the acquisition of knowledge, for no one is going to seek knowledge on any subject if he is under the delusion that he already possesses it. People complained that his conversation had the numbing effect of an electric shock.[1] Since he regarded it as his mission in life to go around convincing people of their ignorance, it is not surprising that he was unpopular, nor can we wholly blame the Athenians —tragic though their mistake was—for confusing him with the Sophists and venting on him the odium which the Sophists had aroused. They held that knowledge was impossible; he demonstrated to everybody that they knew nothing. In fact the difference was profound; for the action of Socrates was based on a passionate belief that knowledge *was* possible, but that the debris of half-thought-out

[1] Lest any reader be taken aback by this simile, on the grounds that the Greeks knew nothing of electricity, I had better explain that the object of comparison was the sting-ray (Greek *narké*), a fish which paralyses its victims by an electrical discharge. The homely flat-nosed face of the philosopher added point to the likeness.

and misleading ideas which filled most men's minds must be cleared away before the search for it could begin. What he set before men, in strong opposition to sophistic scepticism, was 'an ideal of knowledge unattained'.[1] Once they had perceived the way to the goal, he was ready to seek it with them, and all philosophy was summed up for him in this idea of the 'common search'. Neither his companion nor he himself knew the truth yet, but if only the other could be persuaded that this was so, they might set out together with good hope of finding it. True Socraticism represents first and foremost an attitude of mind, an intellectual humility easily mistaken for arrogance, since the true Socratic is convinced of the ignorance not only of himself but of all mankind. This rather than any body of positive doctrine is the contribution of Socrates.

To return, then, to his insistence that if we wish to acquire *arete*, an essential preliminary is to discover and define the aim or function of man: we will not now expect to find that end or function neatly defined in any cut-and-dried way by Socrates himself. His mission was to make men aware of the necessity, and to suggest a method by which the required definition might be sought, so that he himself as well as his fellow-seekers might set about finding it.

In the confusion of ethical thought which was a mark of his time, one fact stood out for him as particularly mischievous. Men's talk was interlarded with a great variety of general terms, especially terms intended to be descriptive of ethical notions—justice, temperance, courage and so forth.

[1] Hackforth, l.c.

I started, says Socrates, in my innocence, by supposing that they knew what these words meant, since they used them so freely, and I set out full of hope that they would tell me, who did not know. When he questioned them, however, he found that none of them could give him a proper explanation. Perhaps in the light of the Sophists' teaching it ought to be supposed that these terms had indeed no meaning; but if so, men ought to be stopped from using them. If on the other hand they have any permanent significance, then the men who use them ought to be able to say what it is. You cannot talk about acting wisely, justly or well unless you know what wisdom, justice and goodness are. If, as Socrates suspected, different people using the same words mean different things by them, they are talking at cross-purposes and only confusion can result. The confusion will be at once intellectual and moral. Intellectually, discussion with a man who is using his terms in a different sense from you can lead nowhere—except possibly to a quarrel; and morally, when the terms in question stand for ethical notions, nothing but anarchy can result. This double side of the problem, moral and intellectual, was what Socrates wished to express by saying that virtue is knowledge. So clear moreover was his own mind and steadfast his character that it seemed to him self-evident that if men could be brought to see this truth they would automatically choose the right. All that was necessary was to make them take the trouble to find out what the right is. Hence his second famous saying, that no one does wrong willingly. If virtue is knowledge, vice is only due to ignorance.

How then are we to set about acquiring this

knowledge of what virtue, justice, etc., are? Socrates, as I have said, was prepared to suggest a method, both for others and himself. The knowledge is obtained in two stages, referred to by Aristotle when he says that Socrates can justly claim the credit for two things, inductive argument and general definition. These somewhat dry logical terms, which would certainly have surprised Socrates himself, do not sound as if they had much connexion with morals, but for Socrates the connexion was vital. The first stage is to collect instances to which it is agreed by both fellow-seekers that the name 'justice' (if justice is the quarry) can be applied. Then the collected examples of just actions are examined to discover in them some common quality by virtue of which they bear that name. This common quality, or more likely a group or nexus of common qualities, constitutes their essence as just acts. It is in fact, abstracted from the accidental properties of time and circumstance which belong to each of the just acts individually, the definition of justice. Thus the inductive argument is, as its Greek name signifies, a 'leading-on' of the mind from individual instances, assembled and regarded collectively, to a comprehension of their common definition.

The fault which Socrates found with the victims of his tireless questioning was that they thought it sufficient to perform the first stage only, i.e. to mention a few scattered instances and say 'This and that are justice.' The type is summed up in Euthyphro, who in Plato's dialogue of that name is represented as conversing with Socrates about the meaning of piety, the topic having cropped up in connexion with the fact that Euthyphro has been moved by what he considers a sense of duty to prosecute his own father for manslaughter. Asked what meaning he attaches to the word 'piety', he replies, 'Piety is what I am doing now.' To his companion in another dialogue Socrates says, 'I only asked you for one thing, virtue, but you have given me a whole swarm of virtues.' He was trying to make them see that even if there are many and various examples of right action, yet they must all have one common quality or character by reason of which they are called right. If not, the word is meaningless.

That was the aim of the importunate questions which made him so unpopular—to get from the swarm of virtues to the definition of the one thing, virtue. It sounds like an exercise in logic, but was in fact the only way in which it seemed possible to Socrates to combat the subversive moral effects of Sophistic teaching. Those men who, in answer to such questions as 'What is piety?' reply 'What I am doing now' are just the men who would say that the only rule of conduct is to decide on the spur of the moment what is most advantageous. Of rules in the accepted sense, universally applicable principles, there are none. The logical fallacy led directly to moral anarchy.

Socrates paid the penalty of being ahead of his time. His clear and direct thinking was classed with that of the very Sophists against whom his irony had been aimed, and he was charged by two reactionary citizens with corrupting young men and not believing in the city's gods. It must be admitted that the most famous of his pupils and associates had not done him credit. One was Alcibiades, about whom no more need be said. Another was Critias, the bitter and revengeful oligarch who came back from exile into power after the fall of Athens in 404, and was largely responsible for the bloody purge which took place under the so-called Thirty Tyrants, of whom he was the most violent and extreme. Socrates's accusers demanded the death-penalty. According to Athenian custom, it was open to him to suggest a lighter sentence, the judges being left to choose between the two. His own suggestion, however, was that he should be given the freedom of the city as a public benefactor. In any case, he said, he had no money to pay an adequate fine. At the earnest instigation of Plato and others of his friends he offered a fine which they would pay, but would give no undertaking to cease his 'corrupting' activities, on the grounds that to him they were more important than life itself. This left the judges little choice, and he was sent to prison to await execution. Once more his friends appeared, this time with a plan which would have made his escape easy. It is probable that many, if not most, of those who disapproved of him had no wish to see him die, and would have been more than content if he could have been persuaded to leave Athens and live quietly somewhere else. He replied however that he had all his life enjoyed the benefits which the laws of Athens conferred on her citizens, and now that those same laws saw fit that he should die, it would be both unjust and ungrateful for him to evade their decision. Besides, who could tell that he was not going to a far better existence than that which he had known hitherto? In this serene frame of mind he drank the hemlock in the year 399 B.C., at the age of seventy.

The end of Socrates made such a deep impression on one of his young friends that it set the seal on his reluctance to engage in the political life for which his birth and talents seemed to have marked him out. Disillusioned in any case by the condition to which his city was reduced and the excesses of its latest rulers, Plato decided that the state which could put such a man to death was not one in which he could play any active part. Instead, he devoted himself to the writing of those amazing dialogues in which he gives a lifelike picture of his master, and develops, confirms, and enlarges his teaching in words put into the mouth of that great-souled man himself. There is much more that could be said about Socrates, but his thought is so closely connected with Plato's, and the dividing line between them so hard to discern with any clearness, that I shall stop at this point talking about Socrates alone and for himself. As we go on to discuss Plato, it is inevitable that we should from time to time be brought back to various aspects of the message of Socrates, and I think it is thus, in connexion with the further fruits of Plato's meditation upon them, that they can best be introduced.

CHAPTER V

PLATO

(*i*) *The Doctrine of Ideas*

WE shall probably understand Plato's philosophy best if we regard him as working in the first place under the influence of two related motives. He wished first of all to take up Socrates's task at the point where Socrates had had to leave it, to consolidate his master's teaching and defend it against inevitable questioning. But in this he was not acting solely from motives of personal affection or respect. It fitted in with his second motive, which was to defend, and to render worth defending, the idea of the city-state as an independent political, economic, and social unit. For it was by accepting and developing Socrates's challenge to the Sophists that Plato thought this wider aim could be most successfully accomplished.

The doom of the free city-state was sealed by the conquests of Philip and Alexander. It was these which assured that that compact unit of classical Greek life should be swamped by the growth of huge kingdoms on a semi-Oriental model. But they did no more than complete in drastic fashion a process of decline which had been going on for some time. The causes were, of course, in part political. There were the disruptive effects of inter-state warfare, and the disastrous effect on Athens—where the city-state organization of society had achieved its finest flower—of defeat and the moral collapse and internal tyrannies which followed defeat. Feeding on these discontents, the prevailing currents of philosophical thought—with which we are at the moment concerned—had played their part in undermining the traditions, the accepted conventions if you like, on which the smooth continuance of life in the little city-state to so large an extent depended.

To appreciate the situation, we must realize how completely identified were the state and its religion. It was not a case of making the Church subordinate to the State. There was no word for church at all, nor did such a thing exist apart from the state itself. The gods were worshipped at festivals which were state occasions, and participation in them was part of the ordinary duties and activities of a citizen as such. Although many gods were worshipped at Athens, the patron of the city, and the deity nearest to every Athenian's heart, was of course Athena, and the coincidence of name is significant. Religion and patriotism were the same thing. It is as if the religion of Britain were the worship of Britannia. The Acropolis of Athens was Athena's own rock, and crowned by her temple. Her festival was the most important in the Athenian calendar. We may remind ourselves also of something already mentioned, that the sanction of law was rooted in the traditional belief in its divine origin. Laws had been given to the first law-makers, as the tablets to Moses in Jewish belief, by the god of the people, or to be more specific, by Apollo, acting as the mouthpiece or prophet of the Father of all the gods, Zeus. Such a thing as personal and individual religion was unknown to the great majority of citizens. The sects which attempted to introduce it never achieved much influence so long as the city-state held together, and in so far as they had any success, were definitely subversive of the established order.

It follows that to question the established religion was to question the basis of the whole established order of society, and that no defence of the city-state could be adequate if it remained on what we should regard as the political level. A reasoned defence of its laws and institutions must provide them with an absolute or transcendent validity which could hardly be divorced from a theistic conception of the government of the Universe. It might indeed be impossible to reinstate the old Homeric pantheon in all its glory. These all-too-human figures had had their day, and even apart from the attacks of atheistic philosophers or Sophists could not indefinitely retain the allegiance of an intelligent and increasingly enlightened community. But if gods in the old anthropomorphic form were doomed in any case, something must be put in their place to restore the element of order and permanence which in the late fifth century was rapidly vanishing alike from the sphere of conduct and from that of nature.

In the field of thought, the attack on the traditional bases of established institutions was threefold: from natural philosophy, from the sophistic movement, and from mysticism. With the last named we shall not be much concerned here, but may note in passing the existence of independent religious teachers, of whom those who used the writings attributed to Orpheus were the most important, whose doctrine was subversive in that it taught that a man's religion might concern his own individual soul and not his duty to the State. The danger of natural philosophy lay in its lesson that the gods could not possibly exist in the form in which the city had inherited them from Homer; and that of the Sophists in their suggestion that the laws of the city had after all no divine sanction: they had been made by man and might as easily be unmade.

These various currents of thought had already been having their effect for some time when Plato wrote. Since he was among other things a practical political thinker, who had renounced an active political career only to devote his life to the consideration of political ideas, he was committed to one of two courses. Either he must recognize (as he is sometimes nowadays blamed for *not* recognizing) that the city-state with all its institutions and convictions belonged to the past, join with the disruptive forces, and out of the different elements that had brought about its downfall build up a new society and a new religion to take its place; or else he must use all his powers to uphold the city-state, refuting its opponents where they seemed wrong, and using them only to add strength to its framework where they were right and represented an element the lack of which was a weakness in the existing order. In any case the two sides, political and religious (or metaphysical), must go together. No real reform of the fundamentals of political thought could take place without a corresponding reform of men's ideas about the whole nature of reality. All this was clear to Plato, and he threw the whole of his forces on the side of Hellenism and the city-state. The writing of the *Republic* in the prime of his life, and his return to the same subject at the end of it with the *Laws*, show that he was true to the same ideal throughout, the ideal of a reformed society based on the purification and strengthening, not on the abolition, of the city-state. Among the ruling classes in Plato's *Republic* the individual is to be subordinated to the common weal with what appears to our eyes an excessive relentlessness. The taking away from these, the most valuable citizens of the state, of property and family life, the communal supervision of their children, the distribution of duties and privileges according to an almost inexorable system of class-distinctions—all this seems shocking to our eyes. One of the listeners in the dialogue itself is moved to remark that those who in the new order are to be the masters of the state do not seem destined for a particularly happy life, since they will have no houses or lands or other possessions but live as if they were a garrison of mercenaries—without even drawing a mercenary's pay, as Socrates points out to make his friend's criticism even stronger than it was. The only reply given is: 'Our aim in founding the city was not to give especial happiness to one class, but as far as possible to the city as a whole.'

The measures proposed were the logical conclusion of the city-state, and Plato saw that it had no chance of survival unless it were pushed to its logical conclusion and deprived of the individual vagaries which, in the circumstances of the time, only gave room for the operation of the destructive forces already at work within it. Only if it preserved a homogeneity, or rather a harmony as Plato would have preferred to express it, based on the acceptance by each citizen of an allocation of function according to character and capacity, could it hope for salvation. No wonder that the saint of Platonism is Socrates, who sat in prison awaiting death while his friends planned his escape, and replied to their suggestions in words like these: 'Do you think a city can go on existing, and avoid being turned upside-down, if its judgments are to have no force but are to be made null and void by private individuals?'

The most pressing question arose directly out of Socrates's own teaching. In his simple endeavour to make men better, and persuade them, as he himself put it, to 'care for their own souls', he had tried to make them see that they ought not to be content with noting individual acts of virtue—just, brave, kindly acts and so forth—but should do all that they could to understand and define the nature of the justice, courage or kindness, which lay behind them. It is not likely that the difficulty which this involves was first raised by Plato himself. It was inevitable that the single-minded zeal of Socrates, who as Aristotle said, concerned himself exclusively with questions of conduct and not at all with the nature of things as a whole, should arouse questions and criticism in the lively and sceptical intellects of contemporary Greece.

The question is this. Your exhortation, Socrates, involves a large assumption, the assumption that such a thing as justice or virtue does exist apart from the acts in which it is manifested. But does absolute justice or virtue in fact exist? The truth is that a number of people have acted in different times and circumstances in a way which we call just. But none of these separate actions is claimed to be identical with the perfect justice whose definition is being sought. They are all thought to be only very imperfect approximations to it. Yet after all, what can be said to exist except the individual just acts? And if your universal justice does not exist, what is to be gained by pursuing such a will-o'-the-wisp?

A second object of criticism was the exhortation to 'tend one's soul', and to do it by the very method of self-questioning on which Socrates insisted: for this suggestion too was one of extreme novelty. Most Greeks were matter-of-fact in outlook, with both feet firmly planted on the ground. The *psyche* was not something in which they were greatly interested. They were content with vague notions, inherited from primitive belief and canonized by their acceptance in Homer, that it was a kind of breath or vapour which animated the body but in turn was dependent on the body for its efficacy. At death the body perished, and the *psyche*, left as it were homeless, slipped out into a pale and shadowy existence without mind or strength. Even for those who through the mysteries hoped for something better after death, it was a new and astonishing thing to be told that the *psyche* was the seat of the moral and intellectual faculties and of far greater importance than the body.

To uphold these novel views in the face of criticism, the two sides of philosophy with which we started, metaphysical and moral, had got to be brought together. It was a task for which Plato was supremely fitted, for unlike Socrates he had a keen interest in the problems of the nature of reality for their own sake, as well as in those of ethics.

In coming to a decision on the central question of what was real and what was not, Plato was deeply influenced by two earlier thinkers whose views we have already considered, Heraclitus and Parmenides.

The Heracliteans maintained that everything in the world of space and time was continually flowing, as they put it. Change never ceased to operate for a moment and nothing was the same for two instants together. The consequence of this doctrine appeared to be that there could be no knowledge of this world, since one cannot be said to have knowledge of something which is different at this moment from what it was a moment ago. Knowledge demands a stable object to be known. Parmenides on the other hand had said that there is such a stable reality, which can be discovered only through the activity of the mind working altogether apart from the senses. The object of knowledge must be immutable and eternal, exempt from time and change, whereas the senses only bring us into contact with the mutable and perishable.

These reflections, together with a deep interest in Pythagorean mathematics, were brought by Plato to bear on the questions of definition which Socrates had raised in the ethical field. For him two things were simultaneously at stake, not only the existence of absolute moral standards which was the legacy of Socrates, but also the whole possibility of scientific knowledge, which on a Heraclitean theory of the world was a chimera. Plato had a passionate faith in both, and since therefore a sceptical answer was for him unthinkable, he did the only other thing possible. He maintained that the objects of knowledge, the things which could be defined, did exist, but were not to be identified with anything in the perceptible world. Their existence was in an ideal world outside space and time. These are the famous Platonic 'Ideas', so called by a transliteration of the Greek word *idea* which Plato applied to them, and which meant form or pattern. In one way then the English word 'idea' is about as unsuitable a rendering as could be found, for to us it suggests what has no existence outside our own minds, whereas to Plato the *ideai* alone had full, complete, and independent existence.

In another way, however, the English word will help us to understand what it was to which he attributed this perfect and independent existence. We say that we have an 'idea' of goodness or equality, which enables us to mean the same thing when we talk of good wine or a good cricketer, equal triangles and equal chances, although there may seem to be little shared in common between wine and cricketers, triangles and chances. If there is not some common ground of meaning when the same epithet is applied to different objects, then communication between man and man must be given up as impossible. This common ground we call the idea or conception of goodness or equality. Most people would fight hard for their right to continue using the word 'good', and would claim that it has a meaning of its own. Yet its use involves a real intellectual problem, and in fact some philosophers to-day, when Platonic beliefs are rather out of fashion among our schoolmen, are very much inclined to question the claim that the use of general terms is legitimate at all. Certainly some of us who use them might be hard put to it to say what there was in common between the bodily skill required to bowl a straight ball or hit a difficult one, and the flavour of a wine. Plato would maintain that they had something in common, and that this could only be accounted for by the assumption that both alike partake in the Idea of the Good. You are right to speak as you do of the idea of goodness or equality, he would say, but it is just these things which you call *merely* ideas, or concepts in the mind, which we must believe to be absolute entities with an existence independent of our minds and out of reach of time or change. Otherwise knowledge is an idle dream and its object fantasy. With this faith one may reasonably go on to seek for a definition of the good, and one will then understand two different phenomena of our world—the cricketer and the wine, say—in their common character as good, by referring them to it as a common standard.

We must suppose then an ideal world containing eternal and perfect prototypes of the natural world. Whatever of quasi-existence our changing world possesses, it owes to an imperfect participation in the full and perfect existence of the other. Since this is an attitude which has something in it of an almost religious faith, even of mystical experience, and cannot be entirely explained by rational argument (though Plato would have maintained very strongly that rational argument proves that we cannot do without it), Plato has recourse to metaphor to explain the relation between the two worlds. Aristotle fastened on this as a weakness, but it could hardly have been otherwise. Sometimes he speaks of the ideal world as the model or pattern of the other, which imitates it as far as material things can, sometimes of a sharing or participation of the one in the existence of the other. His favourite word to describe the relationship is one which suggests that between an actor's interpretation of a part and the part as it was conceived by the author of the play.

We have come to the doctrine, as Plato did, by way of Socrates. Consequently we have met first the

Ideas of moral and intellectual concepts. But Plato widened it to include all natural species. We only recognize individual horses as members of a single species, and have a concept which enables us to use and define the general term 'horse', because in the non-material world there is laid up an absolute ideal of horse, of whose being the individual horses in this world imperfectly and transitorily partake.

When Socrates in the *Phaedo* is made to say, with apparent tautology, 'This is what I cling to in my heart, simply and plainly and perhaps foolishly . . . that it is by the beautiful that beautiful things become beautiful',[1] he means, if we translate his words into a more modern terminology, 'We cannot give a scientific explanation of a thing (i.e. an individual instance) unless we can relate it to the class to which it belongs, and that implies knowledge of the class-concept.'

That last statement is one with which a great many people to-day would have no quarrel, yet they would not agree with Plato in attributing to that class-concept an individual existence of its own, independent of the members of its class, or the constant and unvarying character which is the consequence of independent existence. If to Plato all this seemed to follow, then that was doubtless due to certain philosophical predilections of his own. In the first place, he shared with Socrates those two fundamental characteristics, a faith in the possibility of knowledge and a conviction of the need for

[1] The word *kalon*, for which there is no exact English equivalent, is by no means adequately represented by its traditional translation as 'beautiful'. Since however this does not affect the present argument, it is a question that must be left for another time.

absolute moral standards. And though it may seem to us that it is possible to share this faith without making the assumption that there are eternal entities outside the world of time and space, it was much more difficult to do this at the particular point in the history of philosophy when Plato was doing his thinking. We need only reflect for a moment on the previous history of Greek philosophy which we have now followed—the ceaseless flux which the Heracliteans attributed to the natural world, the insistence of Parmenides that what is real should be eternal and unmoved. There are in fact in the ordinary thought of modern days closer counterparts to the Platonic Ideas than one might think. If challenged, their users would deny that they had any such concepts in mind, but in fact a surprising amount of every-day thinking is conducted as if there were real and unvarying entities corresponding to the general terms which we use. In science, we have the Laws of Nature. Each of these, if not so much to-day at least in the very recent past, is treated very much as if it had an existence apart from the events in which it is manifested, and which are, of course, never completely uniform, nor do they ever repeat themselves exactly. Challenged, the scientist replies that of course these are only practical conveniences and no more than rough approximations to the truth. They represent strong probabilities but no more. Nevertheless, imposing edifices of scientific theory have been built on the assumption of their invariable truth. Without the faith that the same laws of nature would operate to-morrow as operated yesterday, science would make no progress. Yet it is no more than faith, unless we give a transcendental and absolute validity to them. We treat them as if they had this absolute character, while at the same time denying that they have it.

An even better example of the objectifying, at least in ordinary speech, of a general term is one which is commented on in an appendix to Ogden and Richards' book, *The Meaning of Meaning*. It is written by a doctor, and his example is the use of names for different diseases. A word like 'influenza' is a perfect example of a general term covering a set of particular cases none of which are exactly alike. Yet it is commonly spoken of as an absolute, a *thing* which exists in its own right. Even if the point were put directly to them, a great many people would still fail to see that it had not a separate existence of this sort. Yet as the writer points out, there are in our experience no diseases, only sick people, no two of whom have exactly the same symptoms. The general term does not stand for anything real which exists over and above the individual cases. The point here is a practical one, since the careless objectifying of the disease can lead to a rigid and unimaginative approach by the physician which will be the reverse of beneficial to the patient.

We may say then that in one way Plato elevated to the status of philosophical doctrine, and defended as such, what many of us in our conversation and writing unconsciously assume; that is, the existence of something invariable corresponding to the general terms that we use, over and above the varying individual instances which are all that the term in fact covers. The difference is that whereas the ordinary man is still in very much the position in which Socrates found him, of throwing general terms about freely without pausing to think whether he knows what they mean, Plato's consciously held belief that they stood for a metaphysical reality was intended to endorse the lesson of Socrates that we would never get anywhere unless we did that very thing—i.e. take the trouble to find out exactly what they mean.

Given, then, the existence of a perfect and timeless pattern-world, and given that whatever reality we may attribute to the phenomena of the world in which we live is due to their sharing to a limited extent in the reality of the transcendent Forms: how and when (it may be asked) did we make the acquaintance of those eternal Forms so that we can as it were refer to them in order to identify the creatures that we see, or to recognize as partaking of the good or the beautiful any action that we see performed? Here Plato developed and confirmed, in the light of the religious teaching of the Orphics and Pythagoreans, another side of Socrates. I said that another Socratic exhortation which needed amplification and defence was the exhortation to 'tend one's soul', and it was in the doctrines of the religious reformers about the nature of the *psyche* that Plato saw the bridge between the earth-bound human mind and the transcendent world of the Ideas. In ordinary Greek belief, as I have said, when the body perished the *psyche*, now a mere homeless wraith, slipped out ('like smoke', as Homer described it) into a pale and shadowy existence without mind or strength, both of which alike were given it as the result of its investiture in bodily organs. Perhaps (as Socrates on the day of his death mischievously accuses his friends of believing) it was particularly dangerous to die when a high wind was blowing, for it might catch up the *psyche* and scatter it to the four corners of the earth! It was not surprising that in the atmosphere of such beliefs the affirmation of Socrates that the *psyche* was far more important than the body, and ought even to be looked after at the body's expense, met with a good deal of incredulity.

In support of this conviction of his master, Plato reaffirmed the truth of the Pythagorean religious doctrine that the soul belongs in essence to the eternal world and not the transitory. It has had many earthly lives, and before and between them, when out of the body, has had glimpses of the reality beyond. Bodily death is not an evil for it, but rather a renewal of true life. The body is compared both to a prison and a tomb, from which the soul longs to be released in order that it may fly back to the world of Ideas with which it had converse before its life on earth. The doctrine of Ideas stands or falls together with the belief in the immortality—or at least the pre-existence—of the soul. It explains learning—the acquisition of knowledge in this life—as a process of recollection. The things that we perceive around us could not implant in us for the first time a knowledge of the notions of the universal and the perfect which we believe ourselves to possess. But because we have already had a direct vision of the true realities, it is possible for the feeble and imperfect reflections of them on earth to *remind* us of what we have once known, but forgotten owing to the soul's contamination with the material dross of the body.

The basic assumption of the doctrine is that the imperfect by itself could never lead us to knowledge of the perfect. No two things in this world are exactly, mathematically equal. If then we have a definable idea in our minds of the true meaning of the word 'equal', we cannot have got it merely from an examination and comparison of sticks which we see or lines which we draw. These physical approximations have to be studied, but only because they can assist the mind in its business of winning back the perfect knowledge which it once had and which therefore is now latent within it. That is the role of sensation in the acquisition of knowledge. It cannot be dispensed with, but since all knowledge acquired in this world is in fact recollection, once he has been set on the way by sense-perception the philosopher will ignore the body as far as possible and subdue its desires, in order to set free the soul (that is, for Plato, the mind) and allow it to rise above the world of sense and regain its awareness of the perfect forms. Philosophy is, in the words of the Platonic Socrates, 'a preparation for death', in that its business is to fit the soul to stay permanently in the world of the Ideas instead of being condemned to return once more to the limitations of a mortal frame.

This view of the soul's nature, as the ultimate explanation of the possibility of knowledge, permeates the whole of the *Phaedo*, where it is expounded in dialectical form as well as in the symbolic language of the final myth. In another dialogue, the *Meno*, an attempt is made to treat the theory of recollection as something susceptible of logical proof, although the combination of religion and philosophy which it implies is suggested at the outset when Socrates refers to it as a doctrine held by 'priests and priestesses who make it their business to be able to give an account of their actions'. Elsewhere, however, this side of Platonism is mostly to be found in the great myths which form a kind of final set-piece to so many of the dialogues. The greatest is the myth of Er at the end of the *Republic*, where a complete account is given of the whole history of the soul, its series of incarnations, what happens to it between its earthly lives, and how when finally purified it escapes the wheel of birth for ever. The fact that we do not remember the truths which we have seen in the other world is accounted for in the myth by saying that when they are ready for rebirth the souls are compelled to drink of the water of Lethe. As they have just been made to traverse a scorching and waterless plain, there is a temptation to drink deep, and souls betray the degree to which they have advanced in philosophy by the strength which they show in resisting the temptation. All however must drink some, unless they are already destined for escape from the body into eternal communion with the truth. This motif of the water of Lethe can be paralleled elsewhere in Greece, both in myth and cult, and illustrates Plato's use of traditional material for his own purposes. In his own mind it was perhaps no more than an allegorical expression of the actual effect of contamination by the clogging matter of the body.

Again in the *Phaedrus* we have the more definitely allegorical myth in which the composite nature of the human soul is symbolized by the picture of it as a winged chariot in which a human charioteer, representing the reason, drives a pair of horses, one high-spirited and naturally inclined to obey the charioteer, the other bad and disobedient. These represent the brave, heroic side of human nature, including strength of will, and the bodily appetites respectively. Once long ago the chariot made its way round the very rim of the Universe where it could contemplate the eternal verities, but the restive plunging of the bad horse has brought it down and immersed it in the world of matter and change.

The fact that so much is cxpoundcd in mythical form has made it difficult for some people to be sure how far Plato intended it to be taken seriously. Perhaps the best answer that can be given is that which Plato himself gives in the *Phaedo*. There, as I have said, the immortality of the soul is made the subject of dialectical proof, and the dialogue then closes with a long myth in which much detail is given about the life of the soul after death. At its close, Socrates sums up as follows: 'Now to maintain that these things are exactly as I have said would ill befit a man of common sense; but that either this or something similar is the truth about our souls and their dwelling-places, this (since the soul has been proved to be immortal) does seem to me to be fitting, and I think it is a risk worth taking for the man who thinks as we do.'

We may take it that the existence of the Ideas, the immortality of the soul, and the view of knowledge as recollection were all seriously held philosophic doctrines. Beyond that point Plato thought the human mind could not go by its particular instruments of dialectical thinking. But these conclusions themselves necessitated a belief in regions of truth into which the methods of dialectical reasoning could not follow. The value of myth is that it provides a way into these regions, opened for us by poets and other men of religious genius. We take account of myth not because we believe it to be literally true, but as a means of presenting a possible account of truths which we must admit to be too mysterious for exact demonstration.

In such brief reflections on Plato's philosophy as are being given here, it was a problem to know what to put in and what to leave out. Whatever the choice, it is practically impossible to avoid a one-sided picture of the man and his mind. So far I have chosen to speak of a fundamental doctrine like the theory of Ideas and to allow it to lead on, as it naturally does, to the more metaphysical and even mystical side. Since moreover the works most commonly read by those with a general interest in Plato are the *Republic* and the *Laws*, and in them most attention is likely to be paid to the details of his political theory, this is perhaps justified. It is essential to understand the spirit in which he approached his task, and for the *Republic* at least, a knowledge of all the main doctrines that have here been outlined, and of the spiritual outlook which they represent, is an indispensable preliminary. Lest, however, what I have said so far should suggest a picture of him as sitting with his eyes for ever fixed on another world, we may remind ourselves before we stop of the sense of duty which he inculcates, e.g. in the allegory of the Cave in the *Republic*. The philosopher who has succeeded in leaving the shadow-play in the cavern of earthly life for the real world in the sunlight outside, will, he says, inevitably be impelled to return and tell his former fellow-prisoners of the truth which he has learned. Such men in fact must form the ruling class of the

Platonic Republic. 'Unless political power and philosophy meet together, there can be no rest from troubles.' To govern adequately, its rulers must attain a wisdom that is almost divine, for if they are to direct the State towards the good they must know the truth and not merely its shadow. That is to say, they must recover the knowledge of the perfect Idea of which all the goodness in this world is but a pale, unsteady reflection. Hence the long and rigorous discipline which they have to undergo before they are adjudged fit to rule. A preliminary education up to seventeen or eighteen is to be followed by three years of physical and military training. There follow ten years of advanced mathematics, leading to five more years of study in the highest branches of philosophy. Some elimination takes place at each stage, and those finally selected are ready for subordinate posts at the age of thirty-five. Political power will then be for these philosophers a burden rather than a temptation, but they will shoulder it for the good of the community. It is another indication that the ruling class in the Platonic state will be by no means the most fortunate, although in virtue of their enlightenment they are in Plato's view the most truly *happy*.

CHAPTER VI

PLATO

(*ii*) *Ethical and theological answers to the Sophists*

I SHOULD like now to develop Plato's ethical doctrine further by describing another of its fundamental conceptions. The doctrine of transcendent forms was not the only answer, as it was not in itself a complete answer, to the anti-social ideas of some of the Sophists. Another line of attack which Plato developed was to raise the question of the best and healthiest condition of the soul, and to insist that this depended on the presence of order, for which he uses both the word *kosmos*, with which we are familiar, and *taxis*, a word more narrowly confined to the meaning of 'orderly arrangement'. I want therefore to inquire what was meant by this conception of *order* in the soul, and how it may be said to have rebutted the sophistic arguments. It will be necessary first to discuss some preliminary matter, and in particular—as I gave warning we should find ourselves doing—to turn back for a moment to the thought of Socrates. But I mention the theme at the outset, so that it may be kept in mind as the end to which our train of thought is leading.

In early societies, where communities are small and cultural conditions simple, no conflict is observed between moral duty and self-interest. As Ritter remarks[1]: 'He who in his relationship to his fellow men and the gods observes the existing

[1] *The Essence of Plato's Philosophy*, Eng. trans. by R. A. Alles, (Allen and Unwin, 1933), p. 67.

customs is praised, respected and considered good; whereas he who breaks them is despised, disciplined and considered bad. In these conditions obedience to law brings gain to the individual, whereas transgression brings him harm. The individual who obeys customs and law is happy and contented.'

Unfortunately this simple state of affairs cannot last. The Greeks had reached the more complex state of civilization where it was forced on their attention that acts of banditry, especially on a large scale—the banditry of the conquering hero—which successfully defied law and custom, also brought gain; and that the law-abiding might be compelled to live in very modest circumstances or even under oppression and persecution. Out of this arose the sophistic opposition of 'nature' to 'law', and the conception of 'nature's justice' as not only different from man's, but something greater and finer. This is upheld in Plato's *Gorgias* by Callicles, who although he professes contempt for the Sophists represents the sophistic view at its most extreme. He exemplifies it by the exploits of Xerxes.

A corollary of this is the equation of the good with the pleasant, whereby the idea of duty is explicitly denied. The strong man, who is nature's just man, has no duty except to act according to his own pleasure. Hedonism as a philosophical doctrine is born.

Both Socrates and Plato were concerned to deny this equation of the good with the pleasant. It must be true to say, for example, that the orator who in addressing the demos seeks only to please them may do them a great deal of harm; and that the orator who is aiming at their good may find it necessary to say some extremely unpalatable things. But if pleasure *is* the good, it is impossible to make statements like these. How then did they set about showing that those who identified the pleasant and the good were wrong?

Socrates countered them in the first place by his insistence on the need of knowledge to understand what was good—even selfishly good. If we must have self-interest, let it at least be enlightened self-interest. An *unreflecting* pursuit of pleasure may only lead to future misery. But from this—which everyone admits—it follows that some actions pleasant in themselves may cause great harm to a man, even if we still restrict the meaning of harm to that which is painful. This could not happen if pleasure were *identical* with the good, i.e. were itself the ultimate goal of life. It cannot itself *be* the end, though it may often conduce to it. We need another word to equate with 'the good' and explain it. Socrates himself suggests a word which means the useful, or beneficial. The good must be something which always benefits, never harms. If we define it thus, then acts which in themselves give pleasure can be referred to the question of ultimate benefit as to a higher standard, while still maintaining the attitude of pure self-interest.

In all probability the intensely practical Socrates got no further than this meeting of the Sophists on their own ground. It fits his character to suppose that the ultimate standard which he formulated had a pragmatical ring. But on the pragmatical basis one can, if Socrates is the leader, go a long way. Once admit the need for calculation, as opposed to an unreflecting acceptance of the pleasures of the moment, and you are committed to his favourite thesis, which he played for all it was worth, of the necessity for *knowledge* in the conduct of our lives. He maintained that none but the expert can tell what will be beneficial in each kind of action. Hence his reiterated analogy from the crafts. The right conduct of life calls for the same skill in living as the shoemaker must have in cobbling. In the *Protagoras* he is actually represented as defending, in an argument with Sophists, the equivalence of pleasure and good, but he uses the word 'pleasant' in this larger sense. He points out that the pleasure on which we base our calculations must be in the future as well as in the present, and before he has done, he has succeeded in including everything under this head which in other dialogues he describes as beneficial, and which is deliberately excluded from pleasure when in the *Gorgias* he is arguing *against* the equivalence of pleasant and good. In fact Socrates's idea of pleasure as the equivalent of good includes all that in modern speech comes under the heading of 'values', with, indeed, more emphasis on spiritual values than on any others. The possibility of distinguishing between good and bad pleasures, while nominally adopting a doctrine of consistent hedonism, is achieved by admitting the principle of calculation. None of the champions of pleasure were prepared to deny this, yet with it, the so-called hedonism may be refined almost indefinitely into a high moral code.[1]

It was thus that Socrates in his inquiries reduced all the virtues to one and described that one as

[1] The more cautious reader should be warned that the view here taken of Socrates's arguments in the *Protagoras* is not undisputed.

wisdom or knowledge—the knowledge of good and evil. Having enumerated the commonly accepted virtues in the *Meno*, he continues: 'Now take those which do not seem to be knowledge, and consider whether they are not harmful sometimes as well as beneficial. Courage for instance. Suppose courage is not wisdom but a kind of recklessness. Is it not true that when a man is confident without reason he comes to harm, but when with reason, to good? All these qualities when practised and disciplined in association with reason are beneficial, but without reason hurtful. In short, all undertakings of the spirit, and all that it endures, lead to happiness when guided by wisdom, but when by folly, to the opposite. If therefore virtue is an attribute of the spirit and one which cannot fail to be beneficial, it must be wisdom. For all spiritual qualities in and by themselves are neither beneficial nor hurtful, but become so by the presence with them of wisdom or folly.'

Judged by the pragmatical standard which Socrates is advocating, it is not the courage or justice of an act which makes the difference. In every case it is the admixture of *nous*, the purpose of which is to distinguish the truly and lastingly beneficial from that which is spurious because *superficially* pleasant and right. That I believe was the culminating point of his teaching. We shall only fail to do him justice if we refuse to recognize the heights to which such an apparently hard-headed and selfish doctrine may attain.

What those heights are, has I hope been sufficiently clearly suggested. For the present purpose, which is to lead up to Plato, I wish rather to show where it fell short. As a moral doctrine in its own right, there is much to be said for it, but it was not a complete answer to the Sophists. Socrates himself, the reverse of a hedonist by nature, had used the hedonistic arguments of his opponents to turn the tables on them. But this expedient had its limitations. It forced from them the admission that pleasure was not the ultimate end or good in human life. But the substitution of 'the beneficial' still left undecided the question of this ultimate end. It still prompted the question: 'Beneficial for what?' It was indeed still open for a man to take even physical pleasure as his goal, provided he proceeded cautiously so that the pleasures of to-day did not interfere with the pleasures of to-morrow. Again it might be maintained that power over one's fellows was the end. The attainment of this might indeed entail curtailment of ordinary pleasures, a life of asceticism such as Hitler is said to have lived. However differently Socrates might think, on the basis of the hedonic calculus there could be no logical answer to this. Socrates himself might reply, as he does in the myths at the end of the Platonic dialogues, that such schemes fail because they only take into account the present life, whereas in fact death is not the end of enjoyment or suffering. But that in itself is an act of faith of whose cogency it is not easy to convince the unbeliever. Thus the hedonic calculus is by itself insufficient to secure agreement about right and wrong. Two men may follow it alike and yet embark on courses of conduct diametrically opposed, because their ideas of the whole purpose of life are opposed. On this question of purpose the hedonic calculus cannot have the final word.

I have said that it is difficult to be sure where the thought of Socrates ends and that of Plato begins. In trying to describe the more fundamental answer which pointed the way out of the deadlock, and which, like the earlier and less satisfactory attempt, we find put forward under Socrates's name in the dialogues of Plato, I propose to drop the name of Socrates and begin using that of Plato. But not everybody would agree. This second answer is first hinted at in the *Gorgias* and more fully developed in the *Republic*, and it shows that sympathy with Pythagorean conceptions which there is more reason to ascribe to Plato himself than to the master whom he was defending.

In the *Gorgias* he does no more than tentatively feel his way towards it. When a man makes or builds anything, he says—a house, say, or a ship—a more strict description of his actions is that he takes a given matter and imposes on it a certain form. He shapes and puts it together to be a good thing of its kind and do what he wants it to do. 'Every craftsman brings each part into its proper place in the arrangement, compelling one part to fit in suitably with another, until the whole stands forth as a thing of *ordered* beauty.' Trainers and doctors who work on the human body have the same end in view, to bring about a right relationship between its parts. This truth may be given a universal application, that it is *kosmos* and *taxis* which make a thing good of its kind. Thus it may be said of the soul as well that to be good it must exhibit a healthy order in its parts, i.e. its faculties; and in the spiritual sphere the element of *kosmos* and *taxis* is provided by obedience to law, by justice and self-control.

That is the first rough sketch of the idea. In general terms, Plato's point is that everything has a certain function to perform, and that the virtue, or right state, of that thing is the condition in which it is best fitted to perform that function. And all analogy tends to show that the proper performance of function depends, to use a more immediately comprehensible term, on *organization.* In the *Cratylus* Plato describes a man making a wooden shuttle. He takes his given piece of material, and all the time that he is carving and putting it together, what he has to keep his mind fixed on is the work of the weaver. He does not fashion it according to his own whims, but in subordination to a predetermined end which controls the structure it is to have. Taking it from the other side, the weaver cannot do his work properly except by means of a shuttle properly built and fitted together.

It is the *Republic* which completes the transference to the human being of this doctrine that the proper performance of function depends on structure, conceived as the due subordination of parts to whole. The usual sophistic views of human conduct are put forward, and it is suggested that the only valid reason for abstaining from wrongdoing is the danger of suffering wrong oneself in return. It is argued that none of those who exhort men to act justly are concerned with the inherent rightness of the act itself. One might gather from the poets and other moral teachers that all that matters is to give the appearance of having acted rightly, since all they can urge in favour of their views is that blessing will attend the good and the unjust will receive his deserts in Hades. This criticism serves also to reveal the inadequacy, as a defence of righteousness, of the beneficial as the measure of right conduct, even if it were to take into account the benefits accruing in a future life. It fails because, owing to its individualism, it implies that if it were possible for a man to deceive everyone—even the gods—into thinking that he had lived righteously when he had not, there would be no argument by which justice could be commended to him. In other words, it is not a defence of justice *for its own sake.* This defence Plato is anxious to provide, considering only the nature of justice itself, and showing it to be such that the just man must be immediately happy because he is just and virtuous. The question of his reputation, and of what rewards or punishments await him in the future, must be set aside as irrelevant.

He begins by repeating the point that everything has its proper *ergon.* Examples taken are tools, eyes, and ears. Therefore everything has its proper *arete,* defined as the condition in which it can best perform its *ergon.* The spirit of man is no exception. It has its *ergon,* which you may call government or deliberation or anything else, or describe more simply and indisputably as rational living. Whatever the function be, its existence cannot be questioned. There must therefore be an *arete* or best state of the soul, given which it will perform that function successfully. It is this *arete* which we mean by justice. Hence the just man is living in the fullest and best way, and cannot fail to be happy as well as good.

At this point the Sophist Thrasymachus ironically expresses himself satisfied. Socrates, however, resumes the argument by remarking that they have not after all got far yet, for they have not in fact decided what this 'best state' of the soul is, to which the *names* of justice and virtue are to be applied. It is of course this further search which leads directly to the description of the ideal polity, for it is next agreed that it may be easier to see justice first writ large in the city, after which they can return to look for it in the spirit of the individual when they have a more precise idea of its nature. Justice of course, or in Greek *dikaiosyne*, is in ordinary speech primarily a matter of the relations between man and man. Hence the reasonableness of seeking it first in a community. To determine what are the right and just relations between men living in the same community will put one in a better position to determine what is meant by *a just man*: for by that phrase one means above all a man of such a character that he will naturally tend to keep the right relations between himself and his neighbour. That is what is meant by justice in the individual.

In the building up of the polity which follows, it emerges that it is like everything else in this, that it must, if it is to be a community in which men can live lives as full and happy as possible, be an *organism*. All its parts must be adapted to performing their own proper function, making their own contribution to the order and well-being of the whole. These parts are envisaged as three. There is the governing class, whose outstanding characteristic must needs be intellectual power. Their function is to govern, and they must above all things use their specially trained minds, planning and directing the policy of the city. Secondly there is the soldier class, whose business is the defence of the city and whose dominant characteristic must be courage. They will act under the direction of the rulers, who will canalize their natural ardour and fierceness, so that instead of breaking out in acts of lawlessness it will serve to uphold the integrity and stability of their country.

These two classes of rulers and defenders will form a natural élite. The third class will be much the most numerous, and will have the obvious function of providing for economic needs. Everything that concerns the material side of life—agriculture, manufacture, and trade—will be left in their hands, and they will be those marked, as the great mass of people are, by their preference for the things of sense.

Thus the Platonic Republic may be described as in origin a natural aristocracy. As time goes on it will be largely an aristocracy of birth, for Plato thinks it overwhelmingly likely that the children of each class will both by heredity and environment incline to resemble their parents and develop into suitable members of the same class. He adds however that machinery must be provided whereby if an exceptionally gifted child should appear among the lowest class, or one of the highest show himself unworthy to be trained as a ruler, transfers between the classes may be effected.

To avoid misunderstanding, certain points in this organization should be emphasized. The lowest class in Plato's state is sometimes spoken of by modern writers as the 'masses', and certainly in point of numbers it will be by far the largest. But it differs remarkably from the proletariat of which the Marxist speaks, being in fact the only class permitted to hold private wealth. One of the worst evils of political life, in Plato's opinion, was the material greed of politicians. It was an evil certainly not absent from the debased democracy of his day. His aim therefore was the complete divorce of political from economic power. By this means he hoped to get a class of statesmen whose sole ambition was to govern well. Those who were more interested in getting rich were welcome to do so—by leaving the ranks of government and confining their activities to trade. The rulers live a literally Spartan existence, for their system of common messes and common ownership of the necessities of life is modelled closely on Sparta itself.

We see at once that of the four cardinal virtues recognized by the Greeks the wisdom of the ideal state lies in its ruling class, and its courage in the second. Its temperance or self-control consists in agreement between the citizens as to who is to rule. And its justice or virtue as a whole, that *arete* which will enable it to perform its proper function as a healthy organism, consists in each class acquiescing contentedly in the duties and pleasures proper to its own position and not trying to usurp the position or functions of another class.

We then return to the individual man, the original object of the inquiry. In him too three parts may be observed. Unlike the beasts, he has *nous*, the power to think and deliberate. Secondly he may exhibit courage, and it is from the same spiritual source that he feels righteous anger when he sees what appears to him a wrong. The Greeks called it *thymos*, and it may be described generally as the spirited part of human character. Thirdly he has a natural desire for material welfare and physical satisfactions. In any conflict between the reason and the desires, the function of the *thymos* is to side with the reason, and it is then equivalent to strength of will. We may say therefore that in the healthy soul, organized for the best possible performance of the function of living, the reason must be in command, guiding and directing the policy of the whole. The *thymos* will give a man courage to follow out in action what reason tells him is the best course. Likewise the physical desires have their function to perform in the nourishment of the body and the perpetuation of the race, but must be kept subject to the direction of the intellect.

That is the answer to our question: 'What is justice?' in its application to the individual. It is a state of inner harmony, of the balance and organization of the different elements of character. Such a balanced and organized character cannot fail to show itself outwardly in the performance of the kind of action which is ordinarily considered just. On this view, justice is a healthy condition of the spirit, and injustice a kind of disease. With the mind running on a line of thought like this, which is totally different from the one pursued by the Sophists, their questions fade into sheer irrelevance. If justice is this healthy organization of the soul, admitting even of such a precise description as Plato has given, the question whether justice or injustice brings more benefit to the man who pursues them can scarcely any longer be raised.

We owe it to Plato to point out that the supposition of three parts of the soul, or elements in the human character, is not based merely, as might appear from what has so far been said, on the crude analogy with the organization of his state. The influence of each on the other is reciprocal. The possibility of the three classes in the state depends indeed on our being able to count on the triple nature of individual character, which was, after all, the original subject of the discussion. All souls are not in the best or healthiest state. Given their threefold character, we go on to observe that, naturally enough, in some men one characteristic is more prominent, in others another. Were it not for this phenomenon, the state as Plato describes it would be unthinkable. The peaceful coexistence of the three classes, each contributing to the justice of the whole by performing its proper function and not another's, is only conceivable on the assumption that they correspond to natural psychological divisions between man and man.

If Plato based the tripartite character of the individual on the existence of three classes in the state, his argument would of course be hopelessly circular. But that is not what the *Republic* suggests. He bases it on observation, plus the premise of his own that two contradictory impulses, existing contemporaneously in the mind, cannot proceed from the same source. Such contradictory impulses, he says, are a matter of common experience. A man is desperately thirsty, but suspects that the only available water is infected. There is something in him urging him to drink, and something else urging him to refrain. Here are two warring elements, which he calls desire and reason respectively. But there must be a third. When faced with a conflict between reason and desire, some fall and some resist. It is possible (though that astonishing man Socrates did not know it) to say 'Video meliora proboque, deteriora sequor'. The reason needs as it were an executive arm to enforce its decisions, and this is provided by the third element, the *thymos*, that element of will-power which Socrates so strangely left out of account.

With this conception of a health of the soul, based on the right organization of its parts, the Sophists receive their final answer in the ethical field. The controversy between nature and law is brought to an end, for the healthy and natural soul will contain no conflict within it, but will inevitably express itself in acts which are lawful and just. I hope I have succeeded in my attempt to show how far this doctrine exceeds the simple 'Virtue is knowledge' of Socrates without at the same time belittling the achievement of Socrates himself. As an independent doctrine, his may theoretically lead to a life of unimpeachable morality, though its psychology is perhaps defective and it is no doubt right to say that Plato's explicit recognition of the possibility of internal conflict marks a distinct advance. As an attempt to meet the hedonists on their own ground it went a long way. But it was not a complete answer to the questions of the day. These could only be answered, not by meeting opponents on their own ground, but by denying their whole conception of human purpose and building up another from surer foundations. They were answered by founding, in a rudimentary way it may be said, but certainly founding, the study of psychology.

The Sophists, however, as we saw, were acquainted also with the results of the natural philosophers, and based their views on the constitution of the Universe as a whole. Here too they professed to see their favourite antithesis between law and nature. Cosmologies of the type of atomism left no room for any force in nature but chance. To complete the refutation, a metaphysic and theology were necessary as well as an ethic. I wish to summarize, though very briefly, what Plato says about this, partly because I have chosen to make the conflict with the Sophists the thread of my discourse, and partly because it will assume fresh importance when we pass on to Aristotle. His theology started where Plato's stopped, and it is important to be in a position to compare the two.

The theological defence of law is in the tenth book of the *Laws*. First the argument of the attackers is summed up as follows. The most important things in the world are the products of nature, which one might also call chance, since it is a purely inanimate, unreasoning force. The world itself, the course of the seasons, animals, plants and inanimate nature are in the first place the result of fortuitous combinations of matter. Later came art or design, a more insignificant force of purely human origin, and created a few shadows with little of reality about them. Law, and the beliefs which go with it, are products of this secondary force, and oppose nature with unnatural conceptions of right and wrong. Justice is purely a creation of human law and has no existence in nature. The gods themselves are a product of human artifice, created according to conventions which differ from place to place. The 'life according to nature', which this doctrine upheld, consists in getting the better of others and owning no obedience to any law or convention.

Plato's answer is that far from there being any contrast between nature and art or design, nature and art are the same thing. Art is the product of intelligence, and intelligence is the highest manifestation of nature, prior not only in importance but in time to chance, in fact the first cause of all. Clearly a metaphysic which, if it can be proved, will have far-reaching effects on ethical theories as well.

The sophistic doctrines, Plato argues, have inverted the proper order of causation by their supposition that the first cause was a random movement of matter without life, out of which life arose as a secondary manifestation. In fact life must have been there first, and is the primary cause of the movements of matter. The proof starts from an analysis of motion, in the wide sense of the Greek word *kinesis*, which includes change of every kind. It is finally brought under two main heads, spontaneous and communicated. That which causes motion in the latter way, because itself moved from outside, cannot be the first originator of motion, though it is the cause of all subsequent motion. The originator must be something which can communicate motion to everything else by virtue of having the source of motion *in itself*. Whether motion is eternal, or as some would have it, started at a point in time, the primary and original motion must be self-motion. Do we know of anything in our experience to which the definition 'self-mover' can be applied? Yes, says Plato, one thing and one thing only, namely *psyche*, the life-principle. This therefore is the oldest of all things and the primary efficient cause of everything.

This conclusion is brought to bear on the immoral sophistic teaching by the further inference that if soul comes before body, then its attributes must come before material attributes, which means that mind and will come before size and strength. Intelligent design and not blind force is the first cause. To unite in the one thing, *psyche*, the attributes of life as self-mover and as intellectual and moral power was for Plato a legacy from Socrates. Yet it did no more than clarify and develop a tendency that had been in Greek philosophy from the beginning. The Ionians were so far from being the materialists that they are sometimes called, that they solved the problem of the origin of motion by assuming their primary world-stuff to move itself, i.e. to be alive. And there is no doubt that Anaximander and Anaximenes thought it right to call the stuff of the world *theos*, 'God', a word whose associations would carry every Greek far beyond mere mechanical questions of motion and change.

In this argument Plato is only concerned with the point that the first cause of the workings of the Universe is intelligent and moral. He shows no interest in deciding whether there be one god or many, nor by what means the supreme soul initiates in matter the motion of which it is the cause. The existence on the one hand of moral evil and on the other of irregular motion means no doubt that there are depraved souls at work in the Universe as well as a good one. But the good and rational soul is in control. This is argued from the fact that the principal motions, those which take place on a cosmic scale like the revolutions of the stars and sun, the production of night and day and the seasons, exhibit an order and regularity which suggest that they are governed by intelligence and not by madness. The good soul then is in supreme control, and that is all that matters for Plato. He shows a typically Hellenic indifference to the question of monotheism or polytheism in so far as it merely concerns the existence of one god or many. He shows a similar lack of dogmatism about the working of his first cause, suggesting several possible methods whereby soul might initiate movement in matter and ending with the conclusion: 'This at any rate is certain, that by one or other of these means it is soul that controls all things.'

In some ways it will be a relief, as far as the present account is concerned, to turn from Plato to Aristotle. In either case the amount of condensation involved puts a heavy responsibility on anyone who is bold enough to make the choice of what is to be included and what left out, and to decide on a particular order of exposition and linking together of the different sides of the philosophy of each. When one has said that, however, then so far as Aristotle is concerned the chief difficulties have been stated. They are the difficulties of explaining in brief compass a highly complex philosophical system, but one nevertheless which is presented *as* a philosophical system in straightforward, sometimes dry, but always rational and literal prose. The dialogues of Plato are so different from this that anyone who turns back to them after my exposition may perhaps wonder at first, according to which one he lights on, whether this is indeed the writer whose thought has been here described. I have tried to explain some of the main philosophical ideas which they contain.

But the dialogues are as much literature as philosophy, and as much drama as literature. The subtle characterization of the speakers is sometimes not the least of the author's aims. Nor can anyone understand Plato if he does not appreciate the elements of poetry and religion, as well as of philosophy, which the dialogues contain. The value of such productions cannot be transmitted. It lies in the direct effect which they make on the reader. Bound up with this is something else. It opens up another whole side of Plato's thought, into which it would be very desirable to have penetrated more deeply; that is, the aesthetic approach to philosophy. I have said that for Plato it is sense-perception that recalls to us the eternal ideas. This does not only mean that by looking at two approximately equal sticks we are put in mind of the geometrical notion of equality. It means above all things that the philosopher is sensitive to beauty, and from his susceptibility to beauty in this world is led on to the supernal beauty of the world above. Not only reason but the spirit of Eros, the love of all things beautiful, is a necessary part of his equipment, as is set forth in unforgettable prose in the *Symposium* and *Phaedrus*. Platonism is undoubtedly a two-world philosophy, and anyone whose thoughts are confined to this world can never hope to understand it. Yet equally it is a closed book to him who is not alive to earthly beauty, which must be to the philosopher (I quote the words of Diotima to Socrates in the *Symposium*) as the first rungs of the ladder which will finally take him all the way from bodily beauty to beauty in his ways, from there to the beauty of scholarship, and from there to the wondrous vision of beauty itself, never changing nor growing nor diminishing, nor yet beautiful in one part and not in another, but beauty itself, stripped of all fleshly colour and mortal dross and standing out in the immortal radiance in which beauty and truth become one.

CHAPTER VII

ARISTOTLE

(*i*) *The Aristotelian Universe*

ARISTOTLE suffers less than Plato if treated on the principles of the Outlines of Knowledge so much in favour to-day, and such a treatment I propose to attempt. I shall try to explain the fundamental principles which underlay every branch of his philosophy rather than the details of any one of them. First, however, it will be well to give an outline of his life.

He was born in 384 B.C. at Stagira in North Greece, an Ionian with the blood of scientists in his veins, for his father was a member of the medical guild of the Asclepiads and physician to the father of Philip II of Macedon. At the age of seventeen he came to Athens to study in the Academy of Plato. At the time Plato was away in Sicily, which he also visited several times during the next ten years, but there is no doubt of the enormous influence of the head of the school on its most famous pupil. Aristotle remained in the Academy until Plato's death twenty years later. He was an assiduous student of the dialogues, of which the most important had already been written, and made the *Phaedo* the model for his own first philosophical essay. When after Plato's death he left Athens, he could have had in mind no break with the Platonic tradition, for he went with Xenocrates, one of the most conservative of Platonists, who later returned to take over the headship of the school, and their new home was in another

Platonic circle. There was little inducement for Aristotle to stay in Athens. The new head of the Academy was Plato's nephew Speusippus, with whose philosophical views neither he nor Xenocrates was in sympathy, and moreover the city had just been shocked by the news of the fall of Olynthus to Philip. Friends of Macedon were not popular in Athens, and Aristotle was well disposed to Macedon both by his father's connexion and by natural inclination.

The new home was at Assos, a town on the coast of Asia Minor opposite the island of Lesbos. Here was an interesting and sympathetic community. The local despot Hermeias, ruler of a small client-state under the Great King of Persia, had shown a keen interest in Plato's political philosophy, and had invited to his court as permanent guests two members of the Academy, Erastus and Coriscos, who had been recommended to him by Plato himself. He seems to have been in his small way the philosopher-king whom Plato had vainly sought in Sicily. At any rate he modified his constitution by the advice of the two philosophers, and after Plato's death gave an equally warm welcome to Aristotle and Xenocrates. There was at Assos a regular school where Aristotle lectured during the three years of his stay there. He next, being now forty, spent two years on the neighbouring island of Lesbos, where was the home of his friend and pupil Theophrastus, and from the internal evidence of his biological works it would seem that much of his scientific material was gathered in this neighbourhood. From Mitylene on Lesbos he went in 342 to Pella at the invitation of King Philip to take up the post of tutor to the young

Alexander, then aged fifteen or sixteen. Another bond between Aristotle and Hermeias must have been their Macedonian sympathies. No one who was not considered politically sound could have been chosen as the prince's tutor, and as for Hermeias, in the following year he was captured by the Persians, accused of plotting with Macedon against the Great King, and put to death with torture. Aristotle had a monument erected to him at Delphi, and, most interesting of all, composed a poem in his honour in the form of a cult-hymn, which has come down to us.

The opportunities offered by the appointment at Pella must have seemed limitless, for Aristotle shared to the full the Platonic ambition to be educator to a prince, and united the tradition of the philosopher-king with a passionate conviction of the superiority of the Hellenic race over all others. It could rule the world, he said in the *Politics*, if only it were politically united. He stayed in the North until Philip's death and Alexander's accession in 336. Then when Alexander crossed over to Asia as a second Achilles, the champion of Hellas against the barbarians, he returned to Athens. There were no longer any reasons, political or otherwise, why he should not carry out his plan of establishing there a school of his own. Speusippus had died in 339 and been succeeded in the headship of the Academy by Xenocrates. At this stage therefore he founded the Lyceum, so called from its proximity to the precinct of Apollo *Lykeios*. Here was the *peripatos*, or covered walk, which gave his followers their name, and in his own buildings he fitted up a library (the first in history, Strabo says) and arranged facilities for the scientific research to which he was devoted.

The whole atmosphere of the Lyceum seems to have been much more scientific than philosophical in the modern sense. It was the sciences of observation which were encouraged, and pupils were set to work preparing collections of material to form the basis of such sciences, and add to the enormous amount which Aristotle had already amassed himself.

This peaceful existence was shattered when in the summer of 323 the incredible news of Alexander's death reached Athens. The Athenian assembly immediately decided on the liberation of Greek cities from Macedonian garrisons. In the wave of anti-Macedonian feeling which ensued, a charge was trumped up against Aristotle, the old charge of impiety which had been levelled at Anaxagoras and Socrates. With Socrates in mind Aristotle is said to have remarked, as he retired to voluntary banishment at Chalkis in Euboea, that he wished to 'prevent the Athenians from committing a second sin against philosophy'. At Chalkis he had lived only a year when he died in 322, at the age of sixty-two.

The hallmark of Aristotle as a philosopher is a robust common sense, which refused to believe that this world was anything but fully real. Philosophy, as it appeared to him, was an attempt to explain the natural world, and if it could not do so, or could explain it only by the introduction of a mysterious, transcendental pattern-world, devoid of the characteristically natural property of motion, then it must be considered to have failed. His comment on the Platonic Ideas is typical: 'But to call them patterns, or speak of the other things as sharing in them, is to talk in empty words and poetic metaphors.'

Inevitably therefore the dominant note of his

philosophy is conflict. For this, as we have seen, is the man who was the pupil and friend of Plato for twenty years from the age of seventeen. As a young man he accepted the whole of Plato's two-world philosophy—the doctrine of Ideas, the immortality and transmigration of the soul, and the view of earthly knowledge as a gradual recollection of knowledge from another world. If he later felt compelled, as an independent thinker, to give up the mystical doctrines of the Ideas and the kinship of the soul with things beyond, there were parts of the legacy which never left him. Fundamentally he remained on the side of Plato and Socrates. As Cornford put it: 'For all this reaction towards the standpoint of common sense and empirical fact, Aristotle could never cease to be a Platonist. His thought, no less than Plato's, is governed by the idea of aspiration, inherited by his master from Socrates—the idea that the true cause or explanation of things is to be sought, not in the beginning, but in the end.'[1]

In other words, the question that both can and must be answered by philosophy is the question 'Why?' To answer the question 'How?' is not enough. To speak more strictly, we may say that the permanent legacy of Platonism to Aristotle was twofold, though its two sides were intimately connected. What he took over and retained was:

(i) the teleological point of view;

(ii) the conviction that reality lies in form.

He could not give up his sense of the supreme importance of form, with which, as we have now seen, it was natural for the Greeks to include function. To know the matter *out of which* a thing had come to be

[1] *Before and After Socrates*, pp. 89 f.

was only a secondary consideration, since the original matter was something shared by it with other things which had developed differently, whereas to understand it meant to lay bare the characteristics which distinguished it from other things. The definition then must describe the form *into which* it had grown. In that, according to Plato and Aristotle, lay its essence. This question of looking for the essence of things in the 'out-of-which' or the 'into-which' introduces us to a fundamental cleavage of outlook which exists in the present world as in the ancient, among laymen as well as philosophers. Knowing as we do that man has evolved from lower types of life, it is natural for some to say that he is 'after all nothing but' an ape, or even a piece of protoplasm, which has happened to take a certain direction. To others his essence lies in the qualities which now distinguish him from the lower forms of life to which his ancestors belonged. They see it not in what he has left behind, but in his capabilities, both present and even future. What he can now do is the important thing—his function, dependent on his form. The ultimate reason for the choice is probably not rational, and it is notoriously impossible for the one side to convince the other by argument.

Here then was a man with a conviction as strong as Plato's both that knowledge was possible, and that it must be knowledge of form and not of matter. Yet from these premises Plato, as we know, deduced that the only possible explanation lay in the assumption of a world of transcendent and absolute forms partially and transiently realized in the world of nature. From this Aristotle's common sense revolted, because the relationship between the two worlds, the causality of the Ideas, remained unaccounted for. Above all they offered no help in explaining what had been the crux of early Greek philosophy and seemed to Aristotle the one thing above all that needed explanation; that is, the phenomena of motion and change. He therefore renounced them, but the difficulty which they were designed to obviate may be presumed to have remained. How bring within the compass of philosophic knowledge a world of unstable phenomena, always changing, coming into existence and passing away again, never the same for two instants together? Where is that stability which, as we saw at the beginning, the human mind demands?

Aristotle's answer lies in two related concepts fundamental to his philosophy:

(*a*) the conception of immanent form;
(*b*) the conception of potentiality (*dynamis*).

(*a*) *Immanent form.* In general terms, the view of Aristotle is that although at first sight the world seems to be in constant movement and offer no fixed truths such as alone can be the objects of scientific thought, yet the philosopher can, by a mental process, analyse this continual flux and will find that there are underlying it certain basic principles or elements which do not change. These are not a set of substances existing *apart* from the sensible world, but they do exist and are capable of being thought of separately. They are not changeable, and provide the objects of true philosophy.

As we go on to ask what these principles are, we must remember Aristotle's initial commonsense postulate that only the individual sensible object has separate existence—*this* man, *this* horse, as he puts it. The whole investigation is for the sake of understanding this individual object. To do so, we have to grasp certain things about it, we must define the class to which it belongs, analyse the internal structure which logically it must be supposed to have. Picture then the philosopher examining the things around him in an endeavour to abstract, by means in the first place of an inductive analysis, certain common principles which exist (they are not mere mental abstractions), but exist only combined in the concrete objects. They can nevertheless be regarded separately by a mental process, and, so seen, will explain the nature of the concrete object itself.

Seen thus, each separate object of the natural world is discovered to be a compound. Indeed we still call it a *concrete* object, using the Latin word meaning 'stuck together' which is the translation of the Greek word applied to such an object by Aristotle. It consists at any given moment of a substratum, also called its matter, informed by, or possessed of, a certain formal nature. Since perceptible things change, and change was conceived of by the ancients as taking place between two opposites or extremes—from black to white, hot to cold, small to large and so on—Aristotle made use of the term which had been employed by the earliest Greek philosophers and called the forms also the 'opposites'. The reason why his predecessors had found the problem of change so difficult of logical explanation, he said, was that they had argued as if it demanded assent to the proposition that these opposite qualities could change into one another. They confused the statement 'this cold thing has become hot' with the statement 'heat has become coldness'. The latter statement is a violation of the law of contradiction and is impossible, as Parmenides had been acute enough to perceive. Hence the need to postulate the substratum, which is in itself (though of course it never exists naked and alone) quite qualitiless. Given this substratum—given, that is, what seems to us the elementary distinction between substance and attribute—one can explain a process of change—e.g. cooling, fading or death—by saying, not that heat, darkness in colour, or life have changed into their opposites, cold, lightness, death, but that the heat, darkness or life have left the concrete object and been replaced in it by something else. The distinction had been pointed out by Plato, who speaks in the *Phaedo* of the confusion of thought resulting from mistaking 'the things which possess the opposites' for the opposites themselves. But Aristotle's solution differed in this essential respect, that whereas for Plato it seemed vital to assert the existence of the forms apart and by themselves, at the same time as they in some mysterious way 'entered into' the concrete things which were called by their names, for Aristotle they were always in some physical body.

(*b*) *Potentiality* (*dynamis*). In introducing this conception, one must say first of all that teleology as Plato and Aristotle understood it demanded the actual existence of the *telos* or end, that is, of a perfection under whose influence the activity of the natural world takes place. This is not a necessary presupposition of the idea of ordered progress. Ordered progress is a perfectly possible conception without the assumption that the perfection, or goal, to which it is tending already exists anywhere. This is indeed the idea favoured by a modern evolutionary biologist like Julian Huxley: but the Platonist does not think in that way. In Aristotle's words: 'Where there is a better there must be a best', or as we might put it, comparisons are meaningless unless there is an absolute standard to which they may be referred. You cannot well speak of progress, or indeed know whether things are going forwards or backwards, unless your scale of values is other than purely relative; and it must be relative unless there exists somewhere a perfection by which they can be judged, according as they fall short of it by less or more. So at least Aristotle thought. This perfection is provided in Aristotle's world by its god, who is the only pure form existing apart from matter. He is not the form *of* anything in the world, so we are not brought back to the separate specific forms of Plato, which to Aristotle seemed a kind of useless replicas of perceptible things.

To the nature of this supreme being we must return later, continuing for the present in the world of sense. In this world every newly conceived creature must have a parent, which is in two senses its cause: first as having performed the act of begetting, and secondly as being an example of the specific form to which the new creature will grow up. In Aristotle's terms, the parent is necessary both as efficient and as formal-final cause. It is the 'nature' of the infant animal or plant to strive to realize its own specific form, as exemplified in the parent, which must pre-exist. Had the world been created in time, the hen, in Aristotle's philosophy, would have come before the egg. He held, however, that it has existed eternally, and its existence as a whole is ensured by the eternal and absolute perfection of the pure form, God. It is of course only in a loose, because relative sense that the individual parent represents perfection. The entomologist speaks of the 'perfect insect' to contrast it with the larva, but it displays no absolute perfection. If to produce an individual creature requires a previously extant perfection in the partial and relative sphere of the species, the existence of the whole world collectively demands the existence of an absolute perfection. By realizing as adequately as it can its own specific form, every creature may be said to be imitating, in its own limited way, the eternal perfection of God. The inward urge to do this is what is meant by the 'nature' (*physis*) of a natural object. So impressed was Aristotle with the necessity to explain motion —a necessity which the previous history of Greek thought had, in a way which I hope I have made clear, rendered paramount—that he made it the definition of natural objects that they 'contain within themselves a principle of motion and rest'.

Some, as we have seen, had been so overcome by the difficulty of accounting for motion that they had been led to the desperate expedient of denying its existence. Plato himself (though there are passages in his later dialogues which suggest that he was uneasy about it) had been forced by the fact of its motion to declare that the world was only quasi-real, and that reality must be sought in a transcendent sphere divorced from physical movement and change. By the whole-hearted acceptance of motion then, to which his more scientific (and specifically biological) temperament led him, Aristotle was laid under the obligation of answering those who, like Parmenides, had declared it to be impossible. The dilemma of Parmenides was as much as anything the result of the immaturity of logic and language in his day, and the way to escape had already been pointed out by Plato. Aristotle paraphrased the dilemma as follows: There is no such thing as becoming, since neither will that which *is* become (for it already is), nor can anything come to be out of what is not. Plato had shown that this dilemma depended for its effectiveness on inability to realize that the verb 'to be' is used with two quite different meanings, (*a*) to exist and (*b*) to have a certain predicate (to be a man, to be hot, etc.). With this behind him, Aristotle introduced as his solution the twofold concept of being as either potential or actual, a distinction so constantly used to-day that it is difficult to remember how much thought was needed to pave the way for it.

The old antithesis between 'what is' and 'what is not' does not, he said, represent the true position. Certainly where nothing at all exists, there never can be anything. No Greek would deny the dictum *ex nihilo nihil*, and that was one of the reasons why he held the world to be eternal. That, however, is not the situation we have to deal with. An embryo 'is not' a man. The statement does not imply non-existence, but rather the positive fact that here is a piece of matter of such a nature that it is possible for it to become a man. In other words, it is potentially a man. Given his analysis of concrete objects into substrate and form, he could say that it consisted of a substrate possessed at the moment of what he called the 'privation' of the form of man.

This again is not a purely negative statement, but implies the potentiality of realizing the form. All nature is seen with the eyes of a teleologist, and the conception of function is here too in the forefront. The function of an eye, for example, is to see. In Aristotelian terms, it has not fully realized its form and actuality unless it is seeing. If then an eye is blind, it is characterized by the 'privation' of sight. The statement cannot properly be applied to the leaf of a plant, though that does not see any more than the blind eye of a new-born kitten, because it is not its nature to see. If on the other hand a plant is grown in the dark so that its leaves are whitish, they are rightly said to be characterized by the privation of greenness, which it is their nature to attain. Form is essence, or the true nature of a thing, and the full possession of form is equivalent to the proper performance of function.

The two conceptions here described (*a*) immanent form, and (*b*) the notion of potential and actual being—are thus closely interrelated. The view of natural creatures as progressing from the potential to the actual by virtue of their own dynamic nature cannot be separated in the mind from the analysis of things taken as they stand which reveals the necessity for an indeterminate substratum capable of being informed to different degrees by qualities which in themselves are untransformable. The one might be compared to an instantaneous X-ray photograph; the other is an explanation of the process. Since, however, to Aristotle's mind the phenomena primarily demanding explanation were change and motion, it is the dynamic view of nature given by the concepts of *dynamis* and *energeia* which dominates the system and is of most use to its inventor in formulating theories in every branch of knowledge.

We can now approach the question of the Aristotelian God and his relation to the world. Plato in his old age had, as we saw, defined God as soul and soul as self-mover. Aristotle started from that point, but could not rest there, since the conception did not satisfy his conscientious rationalism. His god was not an initial postulate, but the final step in a chain of reasoning which led him to the conclusion that the concept of anything self-moved was an impossibility. This argument from motion may seem remote from anything which we are accustomed to regard as theology, but is nevertheless essential to an understanding of the peculiar nature of the Aristotelian deity.

For every act of change there must be an external cause. We know that the nature of everything consists of an innate tendency to, or capacity for, change and development in a certain direction, and is therefore also called *dynamis*. It is a power of response to the right stimulus, but not the complete explanation of the change which takes place. This demands an external cause or stimulus without which the internal potency will remain dormant. Something else must act in the threefold capacity of efficient cause (as initiating the motion), formal cause (for in natural generation the start must come from a member of the same species) and final cause (as representing the goal to which the development will be directed). You cannot have a child without human parents, or a seed that has not dropped from a mature plant.

The impossibility of self-caused change results from the juxtaposition of two statements. First, change or motion is a *process*, or in Aristotle's terms, so long as it continues, the potency in question is incompletely actualized. Secondly, the agent of change must be already in possession of the form or actuality towards which the object of the change is moving. For a man to be born, there must exist an adult man; for a liquid to be heated to a certain temperature there must be an agent already existing at or beyond that temperature. The statement that something is the cause of its own motion, then, translated into Aristotelian terms, would mean that it was both actual and potential in respect to the same act of change; which is absurd.

This demand for an external mover is satisfied in each separate act of change within the physical world. But it must be satisfied also for the Universe as a whole. There must be a cause external to it, and since its framework is everlasting the cause must be eternal. A perfect being is demanded, the 'best' by which all the 'better' and 'worse' in this world of matter and imperfection are assessed, a first cause to which all the causes of motion and change within the world ultimately owe their being. Such a cause it must be which keeps in motion the wheeling heavenly bodies, on whose regularity depends the due succession of night and day, summer and winter, and therefore ultimately the life of all things on earth. Being eternal and perfect, it contains no element of unrealized potentiality, and hence cannot suffer motion in the philosophic sense, which is the progress from potency to actuality. We thus arrive at the concept of God as the Unmoved Mover.

Before we consider the nature of this divine being, it will perhaps make things clearer to give a brief description of the outlines of the Aristotelian universe. It is spherical, having the sphere of the fixed stars as its circumference and the earth, also spherical, lying motionless at its centre. Within the outermost sphere lie, one within the other, the spheres which carry the planets, sun and moon. These spheres are composed of the fifth element (or quintessence), namely aether, an invisible substance purer than fire. The stars and planets are fixed at a point in their respective spheres, and carried round by the revolution of the whole sphere. Each of the spheres revolves about an axis, and the apparent irregular motion of the planets was explained by supposing that their spheres do not revolve about the same axes or at the same speeds as the outermost sphere of the fixed stars, and that each sphere imparts its motion to the sphere next within it. Thus the motion of all spheres except the outermost is a combination of its own revolution with the motions of the spheres above it, and ingenious mathematical solutions were proposed by ancient astronomers to account for the apparent motions on this hypothesis. This reduction of the apparently irregular motions of the planets to a combination of circular motions, such as might be obtained on the innermost of a nest of spheres revolving in different directions, was retained by Western astronomers until the time of Kepler.

Below the heavenly spheres of aether come the sublunary regions of the inferior elements, earth, water, air, and fire. Each element has a natural motion, of which that of aether is circular, and those of the pairs earth-water, air-fire downwards and upwards respectively. Thus weight and lightness are explained as an internal *dynamis* in the elements themselves.

It only remains to add that aether, as in age-old Greek belief, is alive and sentient, in fact divine, and so therefore are the spheres and heavenly bodies made of it, or of an admixture of it with fire.

To return to the supreme god, we have shown that he must be unmoved, eternal, and perfect. It follows that he must be incorporeal. Moreover, if he is free from motion, and none of him is potential, he must be pure actuality (*energeia* in Greek). We must remember that in the philosophy of Aristotle, with its emphasis on function, the acquisition of form, as a static condition or structure, is not yet the highest stage of being for anything. This consists not in the possession of faculties but in the exercise of them. That is *energeia.* Whereas *kinesis* is the arduous process of 'growing up', or acquiring actuality, *energeia* is the unimpeded flow of activity made possible once actuality has been acquired. Thus the conception of God as unmoved—or unchanging—and pure form, unsatisfactory as it remains, for several reasons, to the religious mind, is not quite so cold and static as it appears at first sight. As pure actuality he is, though exempt from *kinesis*, eternally active with an activity which brings no fatigue but is for ever enjoyable. His essential quality is life.

Of what then does his activity consist? He is engaged in eternal thought. In one of the lapidary phrases which are our rare compensation for possessing only the notebooks of Aristotle and not his published works, he sums up the philosopher's creed:

'The activity of mind is life.' *Nous* is life in its highest manifestation. It is not the same as *syllogismos*, the process of reasoning things out step by step. That is a *kinesis*, a progress from potentiality to actuality which is necessary for the imperfect minds of human beings if they are ever to be rewarded, as they may be after sufficient well-directed effort, by the sudden flashing glimpse of the whole truth which is attained by unadulterated *nous*. God, as we know, goes through no processes. He is pure mind, which can contemplate in a single instant, and does so eternally, the whole realm of true being.

It is a splendid thought, but unfortunately we have not finished with the philosophic conscience. 'The whole realm of true being'—yes, but of what does this realm consist? The conclusion is that the only possible object of the eternal thought of God is himself, the one full and perfect being. There is no way by which he could include in his thought the creatures of the physical world, without abandoning the initial postulate on which all his nature depends. He could not be free from movement (*kinesis*) himself if he applied his thought to objects which are themselves subject to *kinesis*. Thus all possibility of divine providence is excluded. God cannot care for the world: he is not even aware of it. St. Thomas tried to soften this conclusion by arguing that God's knowledge of himself must include knowledge of the world, which owes its being to him, but as Sir David Ross says: 'This is a possible and a fruitful line of thought, but it is not that which Aristotle adopts.'

What then is the relation of God to the world, and in what sense is he its cause? He is the necessary external goal of perfection without which all the *dynamis* in nature would remain sunk in inactivity. Wrapped in eternal self-contemplation, he calls forth by his mere presence the latent powers of nature, which strive in their various ways to achieve form and carry out their proper activities, thus imitating in their own particular spheres the one pure form and eternally active being. God does not go out to the world, but the world cannot help going out to him. That is their relationship, summed up in another pregnant phrase: 'He moves as the object of desire.' In sentient creatures the desire is to a greater or less extent conscious and literal. In the lower orders of nature it can only, perhaps, be called desire by analogy. But it is everywhere the same fundamental force, the *dynamis* or urge of nature to grow to maturity, to realize form, and to perform the due function. And Aristotle's biological studies had taught him that there is no hard and fast line between the faculties of different orders of nature, as there is no hard and fast line between the genera. Although not an evolutionist, he notes as a result of his observations of marine life that there is obviously no detectable line of cleavage between plants and animals; of some creatures it is hard to say to which class they belong. Such observations must have made it easier for him to postulate a single internal force, or *élan*, pervading all nature, sentient and non-sentient alike.

We may dislike the conclusions to which Aristotle was led, but we can hardly help admiring the consistency of his thought. The theological climax of his system is reached by applying the same fundamental principles as hold good throughout. In natural generation, as we saw, the most important aspects of a parent's causation are the formal and final. He is necessary above all as providing an example of the fully formed creature to which the offspring will conform. Since the offspring is created in time, he must act as efficient cause too; there must be an initial act of begetting. But after that, he need theoretically take no further notice of the young, whose internal *dynamis* will ensure their continued development provided the perfect members of the species only exist to furnish the model. The relation of God to the world is the same, with the necessary difference that since the world was never created but is coeval with time itself, no initial act of creation in time is called for, and the last consideration is removed which could cause God to display even a momentary interest in the world. He is none the less necessary to its existence, in a way which is now clear. To recall Cornford's dictum, we may say that in Aristotle 'the philosophy of aspiration' reaches its final culmination.

CHAPTER VIII

ARISTOTLE

(*ii*) *Human Beings*

I HAVE given some account in outline of Aristotle's views on the workings of the Universe as a whole. To conclude this brief survey, the most fitting subject seems to be his views on man, his nature and position in the world, and his proper occupation or function. What I shall have to say falls roughly into two halves, psychology and ethics.

I use psychology of course in the Greek sense of the study of the *psyche*, which is the element of life in living creatures from plants upwards, and includes as a minimum the faculties of nutrition and reproduction, and also, in those creatures which possess them, the desires and emotions, the senses, and the reason.

As with every other subject, Aristotle starts from a discussion of the opinions of his predecessors. From this discussion two main points of criticism emerge, illustrating in particular how his common sense reacted against the semi-religious beliefs of the Pythagoreans and Plato, though at the same time his treatment of them shows that he was equally anxious to avoid the purely materialist explanations of sensation and thought which had been propounded by Empedocles and the Atomists.

The two chief points which he picks out for criticism are these:

(*a*) Failure to grasp with sufficient clearness that the *psyche* must be conceived as a unity, although possessing perhaps different faculties (*dynameis*). Plato had spoken of different 'parts' of the soul. In Aristotle's work this word 'parts' is usually replaced by the word *dynameis*—faculties or powers.

(*b*) Failure to grasp its relation to the body. The others speak of it as something separate, which perhaps can be detached from the body and live a separate life by itself. In fact not only is soul itself a unity, but so is the whole living creature, soul and body together. Hence theories of the transmigration of a soul into different bodies are absurd. The two are logically distinguishable—soul is not by definition the same thing as body, or life the same as matter—but, says Aristotle, it is as if the body were the instrument through which a particular life or soul expresses itself. He illustrates this by a rather quaint simile, that to talk of the transmigration of souls is 'like talking of a transmigration of carpentry into flutes; for just as the craft must employ the right tools, so the soul must employ the right body'.

This is a hint that a satisfactory study of life must be based on a study of the living body, that psychology must be based on biology, a precept to which, as everyone knows, Aristotle did not fail to conform. Even now the wealth and acumen of his contributions to biological and zoological science are capable of exciting admiration among experts.

What then is the soul, or in other words what is the correct description of life? To decide this Aristotle has recourse to his fundamental principles of existence. Living creatures, like all separately existing substances, are *concrete*, that is, they are compounded of matter or substrate and form. The body is the matter, and the form or actuality of that body is its life or *psyche*. If then, he says, one must attempt a definition to cover *psyche* as a whole, we can say no more than this, that it is the actuality of an organic body.

In considering the implications of this doctrine of soul as the actuality of the living creature, we must not be misled by what at first sight might seem to be modern analogies. It might suggest the modern materialist or epiphenomenalist view, according to which life is what is called an 'emergent characteristic' of the body—simply, that is to say, a natural resultant or after-product of all the parts of the body being just so. This makes life both secondary in time and subordinate in importance to the body. A similar view was held in ancient times, and is rebutted by Aristotle no less vigorously than by Plato. To see a resemblance to it in Aristotle himself is to forget his Platonic legacy, the exalted position occupied by form in his philosophy. Both alike insist that the perfect comes before the imperfect, both chronologically and in the scale of value. Hence Aristotle's emphasis, noted in the last chapter, on the necessity for the prior existence of a fully developed member of a species before a new one could be created. Of Darwinian evolution Aristotle had not a notion, and he strongly disapproved of its ancient counterpart in Empedocles. The chicken comes before the egg and always has. So with the soul: its highest and only perfect manifestation—pure mind—exists eternally. The individual may have to recreate his own imperfect instance of it, and so in the individual the progress is from the potential to the actual. But speaking universally whether it be of a single species or of the whole

Universe, the actuality of life is prior even in time to matter (its potentiality) as well as superior in importance or value.

Nevertheless one momentous consequence would seem to follow from the doctrine of soul as the form of the body if interpreted in all its strictness. It is a death-blow to any kind of personal immortality. Living creatures like other natural objects form each one a unity, and their components of form and matter are not separable except in thought. In his own words: 'The question whether soul and body are one is no more legitimate than the question whether the wax and the impression of the seal upon it are one, or in general whether the matter of a thing is one with the thing of which it is the matter.' On the question of human survival he says little, and the natural inference would be that, unlike Plato, he was not greatly interested in it. His curiosity about the present world was too consuming to leave room for a desire to speculate about another. Nevertheless he does seem to have left a loophole, holding that *nous*, the highest manifestation of the reasoning faculty, was of a different order from the other vital principles, and might in fact be a separate substance in its own right which could survive the dissolution of the body. He several times mentions the question and shelves it, as in this passage from the *De anima*: 'Concerning the mind, the power of active thought, we have as yet no evidence. It appears to be a different genus of soul, and to be alone capable of separate existence, as the eternal is independent of the perishable. But all the other parts of soul, as is clear from what has been said, are incapable of separate existence, in spite of what some have claimed. They are, of course, distinguishable in definition.'

In a purely scientific passage of his treatise on the *Generation of Animals*, he actually concludes that reason, of all the manifestations of life, 'alone enters from outside and is divine', because all the others can be shown to be inseparable from some activity of the body. We may also take into account his exhortations at the end of the *Ethics* to the life of pure thought as being not only the exercise of our own highest faculty, but also the cultivation of that part in which we resemble God. In the possession of *nous* he undoubtedly believed that man has something which is not shared by other forms of life, and which he does share with the eternal unmoved cause of the Universe. Probably therefore the reward of the philosopher after death was the absorption of his mind into the one eternal incorporeal Mind. We cannot say more where he has said nothing. The tenor of his thought is better seen in those things which his philosophy excludes. The description of the thinking part of us in the third book of the *De anima* makes it clear that there can be no survival of individual personality, no room for an Orphic or Platonic eschatology of rewards and punishments, nor a cycle of incarnations. The doctrine of form and matter has the last word.

Stated baldly, the doctrine of soul as the form of the body sounds somewhat abstract and unreal. Aristotle himself, however, warns us several times that the general definition cannot get us very far, and that the meaning emerges in the working out of the details. Being primarily a biologist, he plunges into these details with zest. We cannot at present follow him, but, still keeping rather to generalities, may look by way of example at his theories of sensation.

The senses cannot be considered as completely isolated, but simply as different *dynameis* or faculties of *psyche* manifested through different parts of the body. To understand them, he says, we must grasp the fact that the relation of a faculty, e.g. sight, to its organ the eye is the same as the relation of soul as a whole to body as a whole. This theory gives to his views on sensation two advantages over those of his predecessors which become apparent in the details of his work.

(*a*) We know that one effect of his general doctrine was to draw the bonds between soul and body much tighter than previous accounts had done. We cannot understand the soul if we neglect the body through which it manifests itself. So with a particular sense; we cannot understand sight unless we examine the structure and workings of the eye. Sight and the eye are not the same—they are logically distinguishable—but together they form but one living, active organ and must be studied as such. This gives to Aristotle's work on sensation a much more modern tone than anything said by his predecessors. It is nearer biology and farther from metaphysics, or guessing.

(*b*) At the same time his general presuppositions saved him from going too far in the other direction. Previous accounts of sensation, although as I say based on guesses or arbitrary metaphysical assumptions, were uniformly materialistic in tone. Even Plato, in spite of an isolated hint, was unable to offer any better explanation of an act of direct sensation than the action of body on body. This was one reason why he could not allow that sensation gave knowledge of reality. Empedocles and the Atomists, with their rather fantastic assumptions of tenuous films given off by objects, and pores in our own bodies to receive them, were entirely materialistic. Aristotle on the other hand, with his belief in real and substantive form—as real as form was to Plato, but *in* the creature, not above and outside it—can for the first time draw a distinction on the level of sensation between physical and psychical events. Whatever we think of the origin of the latter, we must agree that there is a distinction between the material action of one body on another—as when light falls on photographic printing paper and turns it dark—and the sort of result that supervenes when light falls on our eye, and which we describe as the sensation of sight. Here again a physical change occurs—the contraction of the iris at least—and this supports us in maintaining a distinction between two orders of events—the purely physical effect of light on the material organ and the psychical phenomenon of sensation which in the case of living creatures supervenes.

Of this distinction Aristotle was the first to make use. Democritus had crudely explained sight, with reference to the image appearing in the pupil, as simply a process of reflection such as occurs in water or any other polished surface. Are we to suppose then, Aristotle asks, that bowls of water and mirrors are capable of seeing? It is just the *difference* between the two events which constitutes sensation. His own explanation in general terms is that the sense-organ is capable, because this is a characteristic of all living matter (matter-plus-*psyche*), of receiving the form of sensible objects without their matter. There *is* material affection: the flesh becomes warm when we perceive warmth, the eye (so he believed) coloured when we perceive a colour. The soul works *through* the bodily organ. But other things besides living bodies can take on these qualities of heat and colour. The peculiarity of life is that *when* the bodily organ is materially altered by an external object, *then* another, totally different result supervenes, which we call the sensation. The distinction could hardly be more clearly expressed.

Aristotle therefore calls sensation a judgment, ranking it nearer to reason among the faculties and farther from the merely bodily than Plato did. There remains, however, this distinction between sensation and thought, that sensation is directly dependent for its data on the bodily organs, and so is more liable to have its communications interrupted or distorted. That is why sensa can be too intense; a brilliant light may temporarily blind, a loud sound may deafen. These are too strong, not for the soul's perception, but for the physical organ's capacity for receiving. The trouble is not met with in the realm of pure thought, when the bodily organs are dispensed with.

I conclude with a few remarks on Aristotle's ethical views. What, let us ask, was his approach to the central question, raised by Plato and Socrates before him, of the *ergon*, or function of man? The key to the place of ethics in his philosophy lies in his renunciation of the Platonic Ideas. This turning-point in his philosophical life had even more revolutionary effects on his theories of conduct than on his metaphysics, as seems only natural when we remember that the doctrine of Ideas arose in the first place out of ethical discussions, and that ethical concepts like virtue, justice and the good always stood first on the list of the transcendent forms.

The difference lies here. So long as you believe that an understanding of right and wrong depends on the recognition of a single good-in-itself, which is a transcendent substance with an existence unaffected by the limitations of spatial and temporal events, you cannot regard ethics as anything else but an offshoot of metaphysics. Only the true philosopher can know the why and wherefore of right conduct. Experience cannot teach it, since the facts of experience contain not the truth itself but only a distorted image of it. This was the belief that Plato was led into, said Aristotle, by the emphasis which Socrates had laid on the importance of definition in the field of ethical concepts. He wished to believe in the reality of the object of the definitions, but saw nothing stable enough in the world of action and sensation, and so was moved to believe in the existence of immutable substances existing apart from that world.

And so with Aristotle ethics was brought out of the clouds and anchored in the facts of everyday life. In the first book of his *Ethics* he attacks the Platonic Ideas (although, he says, 'it is uphill work to do so, seeing that the authors of the doctrine are our friends'). There is not just one thing, 'the good'. There is a different good for different classes, a different aim for different types of action. Moreover the aim of ethical study is practical, not scientific; and if our aim in it is to make men and their actions better, then *ex hypothesi* the material of our study is that which can be changed. But where the object of study is not immutable, the philosophic aim of truth or knowledge is unattainable. Truth and knowledge are strangers to the realm of the contingent. Again and again he is at pains to point out that ethics is not really a part of philosophy at all. All that can be done is to give some practical rules which, having been arrived at empirically, will probably work. 'The present inquiry does not aim at knowledge like our others. Its object is not that we may know what virtue is, but that we may become virtuous.' The words seem deliberately chosen to make Socrates turn in his grave. We must not therefore expect the same certainty to attach to our results in ethical questions, nor demand the same rigorousness of proof as in scientific subjects. 'It is the duty of an educated man to aim at accuracy in each separate case only as far as the nature of the subject allows it: to demand logical demonstration from an orator, for example, would be as absurd as to allow a mathematician to use the arts of persuasion.'

The aims and methods of ethics having thus, by the abandonment of belief in the universal Ideas, been separated from those of scientific philosophy, there was obviously a danger that one of two things might happen. So long as metaphysics and ethics were part of the same field of knowledge, neither could well be exalted, at least consciously, at the expense of the other. The danger confronting Aristotle was that either the practical life might come to mean everything for him, or else, taking the side of pure philosophy, he might consider it his function to cut himself off entirely from the practical side and lose himself in contemplation or in unfruitful, because disinterested, scientific investigation.

The *Ethics* is our evidence that neither of these things happened. In the first place, he clearly did not deny the importance of disinterested philosophical and scientific speculation, though it had become less directly useful in the lower sphere. Indeed what it lost in mere practical utility it gained in dignity, and the last few chapters of the work, which are devoted to the glories of mental activity as the highest of all and the summit of human happiness, leave no doubt that if the ideal life were possible it would consist entirely of that.

He does not on the other hand feel justified in leaving everything else and following only this high philosophical ideal, because in fact such a life is not possible for man. If it were, he would be God. In fact he is concrete, of body as well as mind, and this immediately introduces complications. If for nothing more than their material needs, men cannot well get on without each other. Some sort of community organization is necessary, and this immediately involves the moral virtues. 'Man', he says, 'is by nature a political animal.' Self-sufficiency (*autarkeia*) is to be aimed at as far as it is attainable, but the practical good sense of Aristotle is brought out when he speaks of this. 'By self-sufficient we do not mean that which is sufficient for a single man leading a solitary life. We include parents, children, wife, and in general friends and fellow-citizens, since man is born for citizenship.'

Aristotle set out to write the *Ethics*, then (and the same may be said of the *Politics*), from a sense of duty. Science was his passion, and there could be no science, in the proper sense, of human conduct. Yet even the philosopher finds it difficult to pursue his speculations if his bodily existence is passed in a badly governed community of ill-disciplined individuals. For the general good, he must leave for a while the delights of the laboratory or the study and show how reason can be applied to practical questions. Aristotle therefore divides *arete* into two, intellectual and moral, and devotes the greater part of the treatise to a detailed discussion of the latter.

All men, he says, seek happiness. It is the goal of human life. Correctly defined—we see how much of the Platonist still remains in Aristotle—it is 'an activity according to *arete*'. If we are efficient as human beings, possessing the *arete* of man, then the activity which we shall perform in virtue of that *arete* will be happiness. We have noted already that there is this slight but definite difference between form and activity (*eidos* and *energeia*): when a creature has attained its rightful form, or is in its complete state, the performance of its activity naturally follows. That is the culminating stage of development, for which the attainment of the form or state was the preparation. Knowing Aristotle's consistency in the application of his fundamental principles to all subjects alike, we shall not be surprised to learn that *arete* is regarded as the proper state or right condition for a mature man. It is the precondition requisite for happiness, which is an activity, the *energeia* of a man as such.

In this talk about virtue being the right condition of the soul, we might almost be listening to Plato.

But when we ask for the definition of this condition, the ways part. There can no longer be a complete and ultimate definition in the Platonic sense. Yet a working definition must be attempted, if we are to get any further from the practical point of view. We notice when we read it how, in conformity with Aristotle's conception of the subject-matter of ethics, it is no exact scientific statement but just a kind of provisional, rough-and-ready ruling. Its implications can only be made clear by working them out in detail. The definition is as follows.

> Virtue is a state of character concerned with choice, lying in a mean relative to ourselves, determined by a rational principle and in the way in which the man of practical wisdom would determine it.

Arete is a state. We have seen what that means. The sphere which it affects is the sphere of rational choice between this action or that. The word used by Aristotle (*prohairesis*) is one which signifies choice made by rational beings, as opposed to irrational, animal desire. It lies in a mean, or middle point between two extremes. Here we have, reduced to the compass of the definition, the famous doctrine of virtue as the mean, which to some seems so pedestrian, to others an exciting discovery. To Jane Harrison, for instance, brought up in somewhat cramping surroundings of Victorian evangelicalism, where everything connected with virtuous living seemed to be an extreme, it came with the force of a revelation, and she describes in her memoirs how she walked up and down the college garden at Newnham, wondering could it possibly be true. According to this doctrine all faults consist in excess or defect of a quality which if present to the right, that is to a moderate, degree will be a virtue. Thus courage is a mean between cowardice and foolhardiness, temperance a mean between abstinence and self-indulgence, generosity between meanness and extravagance, proper pride between abjectness and arrogance.

But this mean is not a rigid arithmetical middle. It is 'a mean relative to ourselves', differing for people of different temperaments and under different conditions. Goodness is difficult because it cannot be reduced to a matter of rule-of-thumb knowledge. But it can be determined by the use of reason, and there are certain men gifted with practical wisdom who are natural legislators and whose rulings the weaker will do best to follow—'as the man of practical wisdom would determine it'. In fact Aristotle spends several books of his treatise in discussing the application of this general definition of virtue to the various virtues severally.

A man is not virtuous because he happens to do certain isolated virtuous acts. Virtue is a state, and the acts must flow from that state, or as we might say, must come naturally to him. The way to attain this state is by forming habits. We first of all discipline ourselves to act rightly, following the counsel of the 'man of practical wisdom', and in the end become virtuous because the repeated performance of right acts will induce the habit or virtuous state in the soul. The outcome of our right living will then be happiness—provided, he adds, that we are not cursed with any notable bodily defect nor a complete lack of this world's goods; for in these matters he has a blunt realism which is in strong contrast to the more ascetic tradition of Socrates and Plato.

Thus we have Aristotle's answer to the old fifth-century question of whether virtue is natural or contrary to nature. The seeming paradox that it is by performing virtuous acts that we acquire virtue (for surely, one might say, the performance of virtuous acts is the *result* of being virtuous, not its cause: how can we act virtuously if we have not yet virtue in our souls?)—to this paradox Aristotle finds a reply in another of his fundamental concepts, that of potentiality. Is virtue natural or contrary to nature? Neither side is quite right. In his own words: 'Neither by nature, then, nor contrary to nature do the virtues arise in us; but by nature we are adapted to receive them, and are made perfect by habit.' We are potentially good, with the *dynamis* of virtue in us which we may develop into the *eidos* by forming right habits. But everything which is only something potentially is capable of developing in the opposite direction. Its matter or substrate may receive either the form or its contrary. Being potentially good we are also potentially bad. But as men we have the faculty of reasoned choice, and it is up to us to determine which way we go.

The virtue which we have so briefly considered is moral virtue, the best state of ordinary men living ordinary lives as 'political animals'. But Aristotle, as we have seen, also recognized, and indeed exalted above the practical virtues of social life, the intellectual virtue of the philosopher. I should like to end by trying to explain the relations between the two, and to show what it was in Aristotle's philosophical position which led him to admit this double standard, as it were, and double conception of human virtue.

We have seen how giving up the belief in Plato's transcendent forms meant the abandonment of absolutes in the ethical field and a separation between disinterested speculation and ethical inquiry. In Plato the statesman must study pure philosophy because from it he will deduce the rules to help him in political life. In Aristotle's *Ethics* it has become useless to him. Inevitably therefore the choice presents itself: which shall we follow? Do we do best to retire into philosophic isolation, or to plunge into practical matters and learn from experience (which has now become our only guide) how to deal with our fellow-men?

The answer is determined, like everything else for this most consistent of philosophers, by reference to the fundamentals of his theory of nature, and will therefore be in terms with which we are familiar. For the answer is this, that man, like every other separately existing natural creature, is concrete, a compound of matter and form, and his *ergon* is similarly complex. It is his duty to live according to the highest that is in him, and this is the power of thought. But he is not a god and cannot do that without intermission. Hence, as we saw, the need for the lower virtues as well. This dual conception of human nature leads Aristotle sometimes to an apparent, or verbal, inconsistency. For instance, when man is being contrasted with the lower orders of nature, it is of course *nous* which is the distinguishing characteristic; and so the proper, because peculiar function of man is seen to lie in the exercise of *nous*. When on the other hand man is being contrasted with higher beings, to wit with God, then it is his imperfections and his associations with matter which naturally come to the fore. And so even Aristotle's final and almost lyrical account of the true happiness for man in the last book of the treatise does not escape giving the impression of at least superficial contradiction. This true and highest happiness lies for Aristotle in theoretical science and philosophy, the unfettered exercise of the intellect for its own sake. Since it is *nous* which distinguishes man from the beasts, the exercise of *nous* must clearly be his proper activity *qua* man. Yet immediately after explaining all this he goes on: 'But such a life would be superhuman. For it is not in so far as he is human that a man will live like this, but in so far as there is something of divinity in him; and just as that divinity differs from the concrete whole, even so will its activity differ from the activity of ordinary virtue. If reason is divine, then, in comparison with man, the life according to it will be divine in comparison with human life.'

At the same time he follows this up with the exhortation to disregard the advice of prudent poets (it was a commonplace of Greek literature) that it is foolish to emulate the gods. We should aim at divinity as far as lies in our power. And a little farther on he says: 'This part may be considered to *be* each one of us, since it is the highest and best. It would then be absurd for a man to choose not his own life but the life of something else.'

That is how it is. Almost in the same breath he can speak of the life of reason as being too high for mortals and exhort us to pursue it as being the life that is most truly our own.

Now one certain result of these apparent contradictions seems to me to be that though man, like every other creature of nature, is a compound of matter and form, he is a unique sort of compound. We shall never understand the full implications of Aristotle's thoughts about the nature of *nous*, for he seems to have been shy of the subject. Several times, in different works, he mentions the possibility that it might be something separate from the rest of the human faculties and an exception to the rule that soul, being the form of the body, must perish with the body. But always he postpones the full discussion which so vital a topic would seem to merit. Perhaps he was aware that it was for him a kind of religious conception, and difficult to keep within the bounds of a philosophy that was intended to be purely rational. But I think we should misunderstand him more than we need if we failed to recognize this distinction between the composite nature of man and the composite nature of the lower orders of being. The difference lies in this, that the best in him—that which is in the fullest sense his own true nature—is identical with the nature of that which is above him, with the nature of God. We have seen how the only adequate description that Aristotle could find of the eternal and blessed life which the highest divinity must be supposed to lead was that it consisted in uninterrupted thought. 'For the activity of mind is life.'

To deny what I have said about human nature would be to deny both the letter and the spirit of Aristotle's words. The *ergon* of every creature is to attain its own form and perform its proper activity. It cannot and should not do more. Aristotle would say of a horse, as he says of man, that its *ergon* was to live according to the highest that is in it. But he does not say, nor should we expect him to, that this means 'to aim at humanity as far as lies in its power'—to try to attain to the life of the class above it. It has functions which it shares with man—growth, reproduction, sensation—yet the best and most characteristic function of man is lacking. Its highest activity is yet in a different world from the highest activity of man. The relations between man and God are different. Man no doubt is clogged with matter; he has imperfections and hindrances which are lacking to the untroubled perfection of God. Therefore he cannot exercise without constant interruption the highest that is in him. But not even the supreme Being possesses a faculty which is lacking in man, as man possesses a faculty which is lacking in other creatures. We have a privilege and a responsibility. We shall not indeed make the most of these by trying to ignore the body and its needs, nor the community life to which they logically point. For the body is as much a part of us as the mind. Each of us is a unity, as the study of the *psyche*, the science of life, has taught. Therefore in a complete life the moral virtues must have their place. But the moral virtues (and here I quote Aristotle's own words) are secondary. It is the creed of the unrepentant intellectualist. 'The activity of the mind is life.'

Aristotle's philosophy represents the final flowering of Greek thought in its natural setting, the city-state. He was the teacher of Alexander, the man who finally swept away that compact unit in which everyone could play an active part, and substituted for it the idea of a great kingdom which should embrace the world. Alexander died before his ideal was realized, and his successors carved the known world up into three or four despotically ruled empires. To be a citizen of Athens or Corinth was no longer sufficient, for the autonomy of the cities was gone for ever. Looking back, it seems to us that it had already lost its reality before Alexander, yet when we read the *Politics* we see that it still formed the framework of Aristotle's mind. After him this was no longer possible. The helplessness of man before great powers brought philosophies of a different type. It brought intense individualism, and the conception of philosophy not as an intellectual ideal but as a refuge from impotence and despair. It might be the quietism of Epicurus or the fatalism of the Stoa. The old Greek spirit of free and fearless inquiry was gone, and Aristotle's order was inverted. Some theory of conduct, something to live by, came first, and the satisfaction of the intellect was a secondary consideration. The Hellenistic world has its own achievements, but they are largely the outcome of an increased mingling of Greek with foreign, and particularly with Oriental elements. If what we want to discover is the mind of Greece, there is perhaps some excuse for stopping here.

SUGGESTIONS FOR FURTHER READING

1. *General*

F. M. CORNFORD — *Before and After Socrates* (Cambridge, 1932)

A. H. ARMSTRONG — *Introduction to Ancient Philosophy* (Methuen, 3rd ed. 1957)

L. ROBIN — *Greek Thought* (Kegan Paul, 1928)

C. BAILEY — *The Greek Atomists and Epicurus* (Oxford, 1928)

The chapters on philosophy in the *Cambridge Ancient History* make a useful introduction. The most important are:

In vol. IV — 'Mystery-religions and Presocratic Philosophy' (Cornford)

In vol. V — 'The Age of Illumination' (Bury)

In vol. VI — 'The Athenian Philosophical Schools' (Cornford)
and 'Greek Political Thought in the 4th Century' (Barker)

In vol. VII — 'Athens (Stoics and Epicureans)' (Angus)
and 'Hellenistic Science and Mathematics' (Jones)

2. *Presocratics*

J. BURNET — *Early Greek Philosophy* (Black, 4th ed. 1930: the standard work)

W. JAEGER — *The Theology of the Early Greek Philosophers* (Oxford, 1947)

3. *Plato*

G. M. A. GRUBE	*Plato's Thought* (Methuen, 1935)
R. L. NETTLESHIP	*Lectures on the Republic of Plato* (Macmillan, 1898)
G. C. FIELD	*Plato and his Contemporaries* (Methuen, 2nd ed., 1948)
	The Philosophy of Plato (Home University Library, 1949)

4. *Aristotle*

W. D. ROSS	*Aristotle* (Methuen, 5th ed. 1949)
J. L. STOCKS	*Aristotelianism* (Harrap, n.d.)

Post-Aristotelians

E. BEVAN	*Stoics and Sceptics* (Oxford, 1913)
R. D. HICKS	*Stoic and Epicurean* (Cambridge, 1910)
A. E. TAYLOR	*Epicurus* (Philosophies, Ancient and Modern, Constable, 1911)

The few books mentioned here are of course only intended to give the reader a start. For a fuller, and most useful, bibliography see the end of Armstrong's book referred to under (1) above. About this book it should be added that it deals very briefly with the period that I have treated here, since the author's aim is to trace the transition from pagan Hellenic philosophy to the Christian philosophy which, as he says, on one side derives from it. No other work, so far as I am aware, attempts to perform this valuable and difficult service, at least in anything like the compass of Mr. Armstrong's book.

INDEX